The Driving Book

The Driving Book

Everything
New Drivers
Need to
Know but
Don't Know
to Ask

Karen Gravelle

Illustrations by Helen Flook

 WALKER & COMPANY   NEW YORK

For Evan and Emma Squire —K. G.

To Macsen, in the hope that he will eventually get his license! —H. F.

Text copyright © 2005 by Karen Gravelle

Illustrations copyright © 2005 by Helen Flook

First published in the United States of America in 2005 by Walker Publishing Company, Inc.

3 1969 01638 3209

For information about permission to reproduce selections from this book, write to Permissions, Walker & Company, 104 Fifth Avenue, New York, New York 10011

Library of Congress Cataloging-in-Publication Data

Gravelle, Karen.
   The driving book : everything new drivers need to know but don't know to ask / Karen Gravelle ; illustrations by Helen Flook.
      p.   cm.
   Includes index.
   ISBN 0-8027-8933-1 (paper-over-board)—
ISBN 0-8027-7706-6 (pb.)
   1. Automobile driving—Popular works.   I. Title.
TL152.5.G695   2005
629.28'3—dc22

                                        2004058485

The artist used ink line and wash to create the interior illustrations for this book, and acrylic inks to create the cover art.

Book design by Chris Welch
Book composition by Coghill Composition Company

Visit Walker & Company's Web site at
www.walkeryoungreaders.com

Printed in the United States of America

10   9   8   7   6   5   4   3   2

Contents

Introduction

If you're like most new drivers, you're probably very excited—and a little nervous. After all, there's so much to remember! If it sometimes seems that you'll never be able to keep all of this stuff in your head, you're probably right—even many experienced drivers have trouble remembering everything. With time the things you do every day will become so automatic that you hardly have to think about them. But other information that isn't part of your daily experience can be easy to forget. That's one reason for this book.

Another reason is that there are special issues facing you as a young driver that older drivers don't have to deal with. So it's important for you to have a book that's written just for you. Also, since older drivers take many of the things they've learned for granted, they may not think to mention some of them to you. These tips can be very handy to know, so you'll find them included here as well.

Of course, just when you'll most need a book like this, it's likely to be sitting at home in your room. That's why *The Driving Book* is small enough to fit in your glove compartment. This way, you'll have it handy in case of emergencies.

But before you tuck it away in your car, be sure to read through the book once or twice so that you know what information is covered and how to find it. *The Driving Book* isn't intended to replace a driver's education course, but it helps to reinforce the things you learned there. And you're likely to find some new tips here that will make driving safer and more fun for you.

Things You Need to Keep in Your Car

THE BARE ESSENTIALS

There are many things that can be handy to have in your car. But these are the must-have items you should never be without.

LICENSE AND REGISTRATION

Before you get behind the wheel of any car, you need to have these two important documents. If you are stopped by the police for any reason or are in an accident, you'll need to show

them to the police officer. However, it's better not to leave your registration in the car in case your car is stolen. Instead, carry it in your wallet with your license.

Of course, you have this—you keep it in the glove compartment at all times. But can you find it?

About the only time you'll have to show this document is when you have been in an accident. And you're likely to be rattled at that moment. So you don't want to be searching for it under old tissues, half-eaten bags of peanuts, the address to a party you went to four months ago, and all the other junk that has accumulated in your glove compartment. Also, the more stuff that's in there, the more likely it is that your insurance card will be thrown away accidentally or fall out unnoticed when you open the compartment. So try to keep your glove compartment relatively clean and be careful when you're rummaging through it so that this all-important document doesn't get lost in the shuffle. New insurance cards are issued every six months or every year, so don't forget to replace your old insurance card with the most recent one.

AN INFLATED SPARE TIRE

You're no fool—you've got a spare. The only problem is that you used your real spare the last time you had a flat. The tire that's in there now is your old flat tire, which—no surprise—is still airless. Don't let this happen to you. Repair or replace any flat tire as soon as possible.

A JACK

It's impossible to change a tire without one, so be sure you have a jack. Most cars come equipped with one, but in the newer models the jack can be small and artfully hidden away, so you may have to look around to find it.

JUMPER CABLES

If there is one thing that can save you time and money, it's a set of jumper cables. Assuming your problem is only a run-down battery, any passing motorist can help you get your car started as long as one of you has jumper cables. Needless to say, it helps to know how to work them (see page 134). Fortunately, this is one car-related skill that virtually anyone—regardless of size, strength, or mechanical expertise—can master. And it beats sitting in the cold for hours waiting for a tow truck to arrive.

A PORTABLE BATTERY CHARGER

An even better alternative to jumper cables is a portable battery charger. If you have one of these, you can charge your battery without needing another car to give you a jump.

A FLASHLIGHT

Sooner or later, chances are that your car will break down at night. It makes little sense to be fully equipped for an emergency if you can't see well enough to find and use this equipment. Even if you just need a stronger light to read a map more clearly, a flashlight can really come in handy.

A TOOL TO BREAK YOUR WINDSHIELD

Hopefully, you will never be in a position to need this piece of equipment, but if you do, it may save your life. In an accident you may not be able to open your car doors or windows. It's virtually impossible to break car-window glass by hitting it with your hands or kicking it with your feet. Tools designed especially for this circumstance are available in stores that carry automobile accessories. Be sure to pick one up.

THE ALL-IMPORTANT CELL PHONE

Although it's not necessary to keep it in the car, it's crucial that you carry a cell phone with you at all times. In an emergency it may make the difference between getting help or being totally stranded.

Taking Care of Your Car

If you're one of those people who are fascinated by the inner workings of automobiles, you're probably looking forward to learning about your car and how to take care of it. Others could care less how their car works and dread having to deal with car maintenance. If you drive your parents' car, they will probably continue to take responsibility for keeping it in good condition. But if you're lucky enough to have a car of your own—and you want to keep it on the road— you'll have to be responsible for its upkeep. And you'll have to have your car serviced regularly, whether you do it yourself or have it done at a garage.

In order to take care of your car, you first have to know how it works, not just how to drive it. All cars are supplied with a manufacturer's manual, which tells you where the various features of your car are located and how to operate them, what the vehicle maintenance requirements are for your car, how to perform maintenance yourself, and other important information. You should look through your manual at least once before you start driving the car. You don't have to remember everything you read, or even most of it, but thumbing through your manual will give you a good sense of the information that's available to you. Keep the manual in the glove compartment so that you'll be able to find it when you need to.

If you're driving an older or secondhand car, there's always the chance that the manual has gotten lost over the years. If so, you can usually order one from the parts department of a dealer who sells your kind of car. If that fails, your parents, driver's ed instructor, or friends can help you find the items discussed below.

OIL

If there's one thing that's most likely to keep your car alive and kicking, it's regular oil changes. Oil  is the lifeblood of your car. Not changing it for long periods of time causes additives in the oil to break down, resulting in increased wear and tear on your engine. In general, you should change the oil every 3,000 miles or every three months, whichever comes first, and you should replace the oil filter with each change. (Most newer cars require less frequent changes. Your manual should tell you if yours is one of them.)

In between changes you should check your oil level periodically. To do this, shut off your engine. Then, remove the dipstick, wipe it with a paper towel, and reinsert it. Now, take the dipstick out again and look at the level of the oil on the stick. If it's close to or below the "low" mark, add oil until it reaches "full."

A dead battery means a dead car. No matter how well the rest of your car is working, if your battery fails, you won't be going anywhere. To avoid ever being stranded, have your battery checked each time you have your oil changed. Dirty or poor cable connections can also  make your battery fail, so make sure that the cables are securely attached and free of corrosion. If your battery has gotten a little crusty, try cleaning the terminals with baking soda and water. (But be sure to turn the ignition off first.) You can also place felt rings around the post under the clamp to help prevent corrosion.

Know the warning signs of a dying battery so that you can head off trouble before you find yourself stranded somewhere. Groaning sounds when you turn on the ignition or the sound of the engine turning over several times before it catches are signs that your battery may be on its last legs and that you should consider replacing it. Even if your battery has been trouble free, you might also think about getting a new one if it is three years old or older.

Check your lights regularly to make sure they all work. Nonfunctioning headlights are something you're likely to notice right away, but one or more of your taillights, brake lights, or turn signals can

be out for months without your being aware of it. Driving with nonworking lights is unsafe, and you can get ticketed for it. Usually, all that's needed to fix the problem is an inexpensive bulb or fuse. The alternative can cost you a whole lot more, both in time and money, as Tim found out.

I knew that one of my taillights was out, and I really meant to fix it, but I guess I just forgot. Anyhow, I was driving down the freeway around midnight, when the cops pulled me over. Turned out the other light had gone out too. I promised to get off at the next exit, but they looked at me like I was crazy and said I couldn't drive my car *at all* with no backlights. They called a tow truck—which I had to pay for, of course—and had my car hauled away.

WINDSHIELD WIPERS

If you've ever been caught in bad weather with worn-out windshield wipers, you don't have to be

told how important it is to make sure that these little items are in good condition. It's easy to tell when your wipers are starting to go because they leave streaks and smears on your windshield instead of cleanly wiping water away. Cracked or brittle wiper blades are another sign that it's time for change. You should replace your wipers at least once a year, and more often if you park your car outside. Bring the old blade with you when you go to the store so that you can be sure the replacement is the right size.

TIRES

There are two things to watch out for with your tires. The first is to make sure that they are properly inflated. Tires that are under- or overinflated don't grab the road as well as they should and will increase your risk of having an accident. In addition, underinflated tires are more likely to have a blowout, which can be very dangerous. Your manual will tell you the recommended air pressure for the tires on your car. Some cars also provide this information on the inside edge of the driver's door. It's a good idea to check your tire pressure once a month, and that includes the pressure in your spare tire. Although you'll need to buy an air pressure gauge to do this, you can get one at any auto parts store or at many service stations.

The second potential problem is wear and tear. Over time, the tread on a tire wears down, reducing its grip on the road. To see if your tires still have sufficient tread, give them the Lincoln penny test. Insert the penny head down into the tire tread. If all of Abe's head is visible, you need a new tire. All other things being equal, your front tires will wear out much faster than your back ones. To reduce uneven wear, have your tires rotated every 6,000 miles. To do that, switch the two front tires with the two rear tires.

FLUIDS

Brake fluid, power steering fluid, transmission fluid, coolant (also known as antifreeze), and wind-

shield wiper fluid should
be checked monthly. If
you want to do this
yourself, look in
the manual for
directions.   If
not, your nearest full-
service gas station or oil change center can easily do
this for you.

A simple belt or hose can stand between you and
a breakdown on some deserted road. To avoid
this, check all hoses and belts
monthly. Any that
look or feel hard,
spongy, cracked,
or shiny are about
ready to go and should be replaced immediately.
Loose, cracked, or missing clamps can also spell
trouble, so keep your eyes open for this problem
as well.

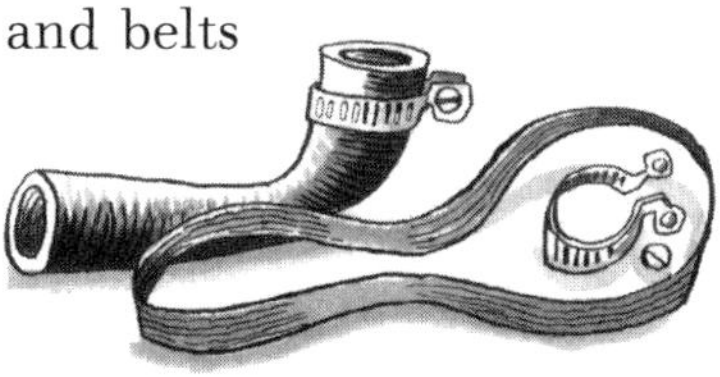

You don't have to be told how important your
brakes are. To make sure they will be there
when you need them, have your brake system

inspected once a year or every 12,000 miles, which-ever comes first.

AIR FILTER

A dirty air filter reduces your gas mileage, as well as the life span of your motor. How often you have to replace your air filter depends on where you drive your car. Ordinarily, checking it every two to three months is enough. But if you drive in very dusty areas, you may need to check it more often.

SHOCK ABSORBERS

You should test your shock absorbers every two to three months. You can do this by pressing down on your back fender to make your car bounce up and down. When you step away, the car should stop bouncing. If not, you need new shocks. Shock absorbers should always be replaced in pairs.

WHEEL ALIGNMENT

It's very important that your wheels be aligned correctly. One sure sign that they aren't is a car that pulls to one side when you're driving. Uneven wear on a tire is another indication. You should have your wheel alignment checked right away if you notice either of these signals.

A NEW CAR

New cars (and some used cars) come with a warranty, a guarantee that certain parts of the car will work for a specific period of time. If these parts break down, the dealer will replace them for free.

Exactly what parts of the car the warranty covers and for how long depend on the manufacturer or dealer or both. In general, parts that normally must be replaced after a certain amount of wear, such as tires and windshield wipers, are not covered, while the basic guts of the car— including the engine, trans-  mission, and the electrical system—are covered. However, the warranty requires that you do your part in maintaining the car by having it serviced regularly. If you do not and your car breaks down, the dealer may not be required to repair it for free.

If you're lucky enough to have a new car, the dealership that sold it to you will give you a maintenance schedule telling you when to bring the car in for servicing. It's important to follow this schedule, not only to keep your car in top condition but also to protect your warranty. You can return to the dealership for servicing, or you can take your car to another garage if you wish. In either case, be sure to get a written statement of the work done so you can prove that you're do-ing what's required to maintain your warranty.

Before You Pull Out of the Driveway

Congratulations! You've got your license and you've got a car—even if it belongs to your parents. You're ready to go! But before you pull out of the driveway, there are some things you need to do.

WHERE IS EVERYTHING?

The first thing to do is to make sure you can find—and work—the various switches and devices you'll need to drive the car. Obviously, you'll only have to do this once or twice with your own

car before you know where everything is and how to operate it. But since every car is set up differently, you should always do this before driving a car that you're unfamiliar with. A basic checklist includes the following:

- Front lights (regular and high beam)
- Turn signals
- Windshield wipers (front and rear)
- Hazard lights
- Defroster (front and rear)
- Air conditioner
- Heater
- Gas cover release lever
- Hood release lever
- Music system
- Windows
- Door locks

The next step is to check the gear selector to see how it's set up. You'll find it in one of two places—on the steering column or on the floor between the driver's and passenger's seats. Most cars these days have automatic transmissions, and in this case a simple look should be enough. If you're driving a car with a manual transmission, you should actually try shifting into all the gears. Some gears may require you to press down while shifting, and it's better to know this before you need to do it. You also need to find and test the clutch.

DOES EVERYTHING FIT?

Check to see that the seat is the right distance from the steering wheel, gas pedal, and brakes for your arms and legs to reach comfortably. Then, check the interior and exterior rearview mirrors. Are they correctly positioned for you? Even if no one uses the car except you, don't assume that

the mirrors will be in the same position that you left them in. Exterior mirrors can easily be knocked out of position by a car or pedestrian passing too close to the side of your car, and you yourself may have knocked the interior mirror off-center while reaching for something as you left the car. In any event, trying to adjust the seat, the rearview mirror, or the exterior side mirrors while the car is moving is difficult and dangerous as Alana discovered.

> I'm very short, and my brother's pretty tall. He was the last one to drive the car, so the seat was too far back for me; but I didn't really notice until I'd gone a block or so. It never occurred to me not to try to change it while I was driving. But when I pulled the release, instead of going forward, the seat shot all the way back! I couldn't even reach the pedals. It was really lucky that I was going slow and there were no other cars around because I had to drive into a hedge to stop.

GET YOUR SOUNDS TOGETHER

Preset your radio so that the most you have to do to change the station is to press a button. Also, decide what CDs you want to listen to before you get in the car so that you're not fumbling through a stack while you're driving. If you don't have an automatic CD changer on your system, don't change them until you have stopped. Finally, do not wear headphones while you're driving. It will make it hard—or impossible—for you to hear sirens or the warning honk from another driver.

GET SECURE

Fasten your seat belt! And make sure that your passengers do too. Two-thirds of the people who have died in car accidents were not wearing seat belts. So don't start the car until everyone has buckled up. It's also a good idea to lock your door. Along with wearing a seat belt, this can reduce the chance of your being  thrown out of the car in an accident. Locking your door also cuts down on your risk of being carjacked.

Hitting the Road

SOME ALL-PURPOSE DRIVING TIPS

The chapters that follow will give you some advice about driving under specific conditions. But here are some all-purpose tips that apply anytime and anywhere.

GIVE YOURSELF TIME

Being under pressure to get somewhere can cause you to be preoccupied, to take chances, or to drive faster than you should. Give yourself a break by allowing extra time to get where you're going.

PAY ATTENTION

Distractions are a primary cause of accidents. Talking to passengers or on your cell phone, eating, changing a CD, or just worrying about your next math test can all take your mind off the road ahead, so do your best to eliminate distractions and focus solely on driving. Controlling a 2,000- to 4,000-pound vehicle is a full-time job that requires everything you've got.

DON'T SPEED!

You've heard it a million times, but it's true—speed kills! Thirty-seven percent of all sixteen-year-old drivers involved in fatal crashes were speeding. And dying may not be your only worry: in a typical year, 6,800 spinal-cord injuries, 179,000 brain injuries, and 630,000 facial injuries occur as a result of car accidents in the United States. Remember, everyone thinks it can't happen to them until it does, so slow down.

CREATE A SPACE CUSHION

Give yourself a space cushion. As a general rule, try to leave space around your vehicle, especially in front, but on the sides as well. This cushion will give you more options if something unexpected happens.

BE AWARE OF OTHER DRIVERS

Observe what other drivers around you are doing. Notice the drivers on either side of you, as well as in front and in back of you. Never assume that

they are going to do what you expect them to, what they should do, or even what they started to do. Alex learned this the hard way when he was twenty-five and had been driving in Los Angeles for several years.

It was early in the afternoon and I was coming up an entrance ramp to the freeway. The traffic wasn't bad, and there was only one car in front of me on the ramp. There was plenty of room for both of us to get on, so I assumed she'd just go ahead and go. I took a quick look behind me to make sure it was okay and hit the accelerator.

Unfortunately, while he was glancing back at the oncoming traffic, the woman in front of him stopped dead in her tracks.

Wham! I slammed right into her. Knocked her onto the freeway like a billiard ball. Counting both of us, it caused a five-car pileup. Luckily, nobody died. But my insurance was messed up for years.

CHECK YOUR BLIND SPOT

You probably already know that there is a blind spot—an area that isn't visible through your side mirrors—on the right-hand and the left-hand sides of your car, but it can be easy to forget this. Not checking your blind spot can result in a collision with an unseen car beside you, so turn your head and take a quick look through the side window every time you change lanes, to make sure there's no one there.

COMBAT GLARE

Glare can be caused by many things, including the headlights of other cars, dirt on your windshield, driving into the sun at dusk or dawn, and driving through snow-covered landscapes. To cut down on glare, wear sunglasses during the day, use your sun visor, and keep your windows clean. And if you're having trouble seeing, slow down so that you can stop quickly if you need to.

BEWARE OF FATIGUE

Being tired slows your reaction time and affects your ability to make decisions. To avoid becoming drowsy when you're driving, take breaks and keep the inside of your car cool. If you feel yourself drifting off while at the wheel, pull over immediately. Take a quick nap, sing along with your music, chew some gum, or get out of the car and walk around for a while to wake yourself up.

TAKE CARE AT INTERSECTIONS

Countless accidents happen because a driver tries to sneak through an intersection after the light turns red or before it turns green. Clearly, this is a dumb idea and something that you wouldn't dream of doing. However, even if the light is

green, scan the intersection before you enter it. You never know when someone will be there who shouldn't.

HAVE AN ESCAPE ROUTE

Always try to have an escape route planned in case you need one. For example, some people make a point of driving in the lane next to a grassy divider. This way they have a place to go if something happens ahead. Others always pick the middle lane on a three-lane road because they like being able to move either right or left in an emergency. What's important is not what your plan is, but that you have one (or several) that you think will work for you.

Getting Gas

Getting gas may be one of the easiest things involved in driving a car. Still, there are a few things you should be aware of before pulling up to the pump.

WHAT GRADE?

As you probably already know, gasoline comes in several different grades or octanes—87 (regular), 89 (plus), and 93 (super or premium)—increasing in price from the lowest to the highest grade. Most cars run well on regular gasoline, while high-performance and large cars usually do better with a higher grade. The owner's manual for your car will tell you what grade you should use. It's a good idea to follow this advice. Generally, using a higher grade of gas than recommended will not make a noticeable difference in how your car runs, but it will definitely make a difference in how much you pay. On the other hand, you may be able to get away with using a lower grade than recommended, but this will depend on your car and the kind of driving you do.

FULL-SERVICE AND SELF-SERVICE STATIONS

At full-service stations the attendant will pump the gas for you. All you have to do is to tell him what grade of gas you want and how much gas to give you. Attendants at full-service stations will also clean your windshield and check your oil and water, but you may have to ask them to do this. You can buy oil, transmission fluid, and brake fluid here as well. Some full-service stations also

have bathrooms, and some have air pumps for re-filling your tires. Almost all accept both cash and credit cards.

In New Jersey and Oregon, only full-service stations are permitted by law. Everywhere else, full-service stations are becoming fewer and fewer, and in some areas, you might not be able to find any at all. Most stations now are self-service, which means that you must do everything, including refilling your gas tank, checking your oil and other fluid levels, and cleaning your windshield. Although most self-service gas stations accept both cash and credit cards, some—particularly those open late at night—may take credit cards only.

Many self-service stations are combined with a convenience store. They carry milk, soda, and snacks, but if you need oil, transmission fluid, or brake fluid, you may be out of luck. Others are simply a number

of gas pumps with a shelter in the middle for the attendant and the register. These often do not have a public bathroom, so keep this in mind when looking for a place to take a break.

More often than not, you're going to have to pump your own gas. The first step in doing this is to learn—and remember—what side of the car your gas tank is on. The hoses on most gas pumps are relatively short, so you'll have to pull up to a pump that's on the same side as your tank. Turn your engine off, and if you smoke, put your cigarette out. Before getting out of the car, flip the lever that opens the cover of your gas tank. (It's usually located on the floor next to the driver's seat.)

If the pump takes credit cards and you have one, all you have to do is insert the card in the slot, answer the questions on the screen above, choose the grade of gas that you want, put the nozzle of the hose into your tank, press the start but-ton on the pump, and squeeze the handle on the noz-zle. If the pump doesn't have a start button, lift the cradle that the hose sits in to start the pump, then squeeze the handle to get the gas flowing. If nothing happens, chances are that you've done one of two things: either you forgot to push the start button or lift the cradle or you don't have the nozzle all the way into your tank. The gas pump will shut off automatically when your tank is full, but you can stop anytime before then by releasing your grip on the handle. It's easy to forget and leave your gas cap on top of the car, so be sure to check that you've put it back on before driving away.

The process is the same if the pump doesn't take credit cards or you want to use cash. But in this case, you'll have to pay the attendant. Some stations will let you pump the gas first and then pay, saving you from making extra trips to the attendant. At others you'll have to give the attendant money or a credit card first, go back to your car and pump your gas, then return to the attendant to get your change or your credit card.

One final tip—if you don't have a credit card, you may want to ask your parents for one, even if you're allowed to use it for emergency fuel only. That way you're covered if you don't have enough gas to drive to the next station or if the only station open doesn't accept cash.

Driving in Bad Weather

Bad weather dramatically increases the difficulty of driving and the possibility that you will run into trouble while behind the wheel. Although each type of weather presents its own special hazards, whenever the weather worsens you must stay super-alert. Be especially aware of your surroundings, and drive as if something unexpected is going to happen.

POOR VISIBILITY

Rain, snow, sleet, fog, and sandstorms all have one thing in common: all result in poor—or some-

times zero—visibility. At the bare minimum, this means you must slow down. This is the safe thing to do, and besides, you can get a ticket if you don't. Legal speed limits change in bad weather. The posted limits assume that driving conditions are good, or at least acceptable. When conditions worsen, police can ticket you for reckless driving even if you're going under the posted limit. Driving more slowly means that it will take you longer to get where you're going, so you should also allow yourself more time.

Although poor visibility increases the risks of driving no matter where you are, it causes special problems at intersections. When drivers have trouble seeing stop signs, reading street names, or spotting approaching cars, they tend to nose into the intersection and inch their way across. So when crossing an intersection, be aware that other drivers may stray into your path. Storms of any kind, especially when accompanied by high winds, can cause traffic lights to go out. Needless to say, when no one knows whose turn it is, the probability of accidents increases, so be especially careful under these circumstances.

Even animals looking for shelter can easily become disoriented when visibility is poor. If there's snow covering the road, creatures that are usually careful around cars can end up in the middle of the street without knowing it. So regardless of whether you're driving in the city, the suburbs, or the country, you'll need to keep your eyes open for wandering critters as well.

Poor visibility is one thing, but if you can't see at all, you need to get off the road. You wouldn't think of driving with a blindfold on, so it doesn't make sense to drive under these conditions either. Find a place that's wide enough to pull over safely, turn on your hazard lights so that you won't be rear-ended by the next person who can't see, and wait until conditions improve, even if that takes a while. Whatever time you lose will be less than the time it takes to recover from an accident.

Finally, in situations with reduced visibility, it's even more important to be able to hear what's going on around you. If you're playing music, keep it low so that it won't drown out the sound of another car's horn, a truck trying to pass you, or the arrival of an emergency road service vehicle. Snow muffles outside sounds, so it's especially important to keep the noise down inside your car when it's snowing.

In addition to causing poor visibility, rain can make roads very slippery. Asphalt becomes especially slick when water forms a film over the surface, causing cars to hydroplane, or skim across the top of the water. This can happen most often when it has just started to rain and during a heavy rainstorm. It takes a while for rain to soak into the pavement, and until this happens, the water collects on the surface, forming a thin film over the road. In heavy rain the pavement is saturated and cannot absorb more water, so the excess accumulates in a sheet on top of the road. Either way, this layer of water keeps your tires from making contact with the pavement, and without good tire traction you'll have a hard time controlling your car.

Rain can also make fallen leaves very slippery, so be especially careful when there are leaves on the road. Even if the top layer appears dry, the leaves underneath may be wet or partially decayed, making them much slicker than they look.

Another reason to avoid driving in heavy rain

is that water can get under your hood, affecting your wiring and causing your car to malfunction. It's easy for this to happen when rain is being driven sideways by the wind or when you drive through standing water that is too deep.

FLOODING

The type of flooding that most drivers encounter occurs when heavy rains leave standing water on the roads. This water may be in deep pools here and there, or it may cover the road entirely in places. The problem is figuring out whether you can safely drive through it. Generally, you should be able to make it through if the water level does not go above your hub caps and if you drive slowly. Barreling through water can force it into your engine, messing up your wiring and leaving you with a car that's literally "dead in the water." Once you're out of the water, test your brakes once or twice to make sure they're working correctly.

A more serious risk is trying to drive through flowing water. You've probably seen news reports of drivers who had to be rescued when their cars were swept away by currents that were much stronger than they appeared. To his surprise, Max found that being in an SUV is no guarantee that this won't happen.

I was driving down this little valley near my house. It had been raining a lot over the past week, and the creek at the bottom had risen so much that it covered the road in a couple of places. I didn't think much of it, because I've lived here all my life and I've seen this plenty of times. Besides, I had an SUV with four-wheel drive, and they're supposed to be able to deal with anything, so I just kept on going. In one place the overflow had caused part of the road to cave in; but I couldn't tell, because of all the water. I drove right into this big hole and couldn't get out. Meanwhile, it started to rain again. In less than an hour the water was up to my windows and the current had gotten really strong. Fortunately, some guy came along and helped me get across the creek, but I had to leave my car. When I came back the next day, it was about a quarter mile downstream, completely submerged.

Take a tip from Max and use your head when trying to cross a current, particularly in parts of the country where flash floods are common. Be especially wary of fast-flowing currents, even if they don't seem very deep. If something tells you that it's not a good idea to drive through flowing water, it probably isn't.

WIND

Assuming you have the sense not to be out in a hurricane or tornado, the usual problem with high winds is that they blow rain, snow, sleet, sand, or debris into your windshield, reducing visibility. An even more dangerous situation occurs when really heavy winds blow electrical wires or tree limbs down. *Never* try to move a downed electrical wire from your car or the road in front of you. As long as you stay in your car, the rubber tires will usually insulate you from electrical shock. If you can't drive around the wire, either back up and turn around or stay put. Of course, if you have a cell phone with you, you should call 911 for help.

SNOW

If possible, don't go out until the roads have been plowed or salted or both, and even then, drive slowly and carefully. However, if you have to drive while it's still snowing, keep the following tips in mind. During a snowstorm, snow may cover the

lane markings, making it hard for you to know if you're in a lane or not. Slow down and try to stay in the tracks of the car in front of you. Other cars will be doing the same, so it won't really matter if you're in a lane or not. Also, it's usually easier to drive in a path made by another car than to try to forge your own way through the snow.

When the snow is deep, both people and animals tend to walk in the road. Streets are usually plowed before sidewalks are shoveled, and even if the plow hasn't come through, traffic forms a pathway that's easier to walk on. Be aware that a pedestrian may suddenly slip in front of you. Since it is much harder to stop quickly on snow or ice, drive very slowly when there are people or animals in the road.

Snow, slush, and ice can make the road very slippery, and it's easy to skid into another car or off the road. Under these conditions, you can slide into a snowbank and become stuck. You may have to be towed, and it can be hours before someone can get to you. If your exhaust pipe or muffler is blocked by snow, keeping your engine or heater on to stay warm can result in quick death from carbon monoxide poisoning. If you need to keep the engine going, make sure that your muffler is clear and crack your window slightly to get fresh air. Check your muffler periodically if it continues to snow, since it may get buried as the snow gets deeper. If you're stranded and waiting for help, try to keep your windows from fogging over. Otherwise, rescue personnel who are unable to see you may think your car is empty.

A final word to the wise—if you are only going a short distance from your house to a friend's or the store, it can be tempting not to bother wearing boots and a heavy coat. After all, there's a heater in the car and you're only going a few miles down the road. However, if you break down, slide into a snowbank, or get into an accident, you'll be mighty cold in just those sneakers and a jacket.

ICE OR SLEET

Ice or Sleet Storms

Ice or sleet storms result in extremely slippery road conditions, so make every effort to avoid driving in this weather. In addition, when ice coats electrical wires and tree limbs, the additional weight can cause them to snap and fall. Again, *never* try to move downed electrical cables. And even when you're safe at home, protect your car from falling tree limbs if you can by making sure it's in the garage or under a carport.

Black Ice

This type of ice is particularly dangerous because it's so hard to see. Black ice occurs when ice or slush melts and refreezes over and over again. In the process the ice picks up the dirt on the road and soon looks just like the pavement. If you've had a series of days when ice or slush has melted and refrozen, be alert for black-ice patches on the road.

F O G

Dense fog is one of the most difficult and dangerous conditions to drive in because it can make it impossible for you to see anything at all. Under these conditions, using your high beams may seem like an obvious thing to do to increase visibility. But this is actually a bad idea when driving in fog. Because of the angle, light from your high beams will bounce off the fog and back into your eyes.

Although you should pull off the road and turn on your hazard lights anytime you can't see, this is particularly true in foggy conditions. If the fog is really thick, you may even have to get out of the car and look to make sure that you're safely off the pavement. Be extremely careful when getting out of a car under these circumstances, and be sure to get out on the side *away* from the road. Other drivers will have a hard enough time spotting your car—they're even less likely to be able to see you.

EXTREME TEMPERATURES

Extreme temperatures can affect your car in several ways. In very cold weather batteries tend to die, while in very hot weather cars are more likely to overheat. Tubes that carry fluid or air—such as the lines for gas, brake fluid, and transmission fluid—are especially vulnerable to extreme temperatures, and can freeze and crack in cold weather or expand and burst when it's hot. Regular servicing is the best way to avoid temperature-related problems. At the very least, you

should have your battery, wiring, connecting cables, fluid and air tubes, air conditioner, heater, and tires checked at each change of season. And in the fall and spring, make sure the radiator is full and has the right mixture of coolant and water for the climate in which you live. Consult your owner's manual as to how often to replace the fluid.

There are two other seasonal problems that are worth mentioning. In the winter, snow, ice, and freezing temperatures result in more and bigger potholes, making the roads much bumpier. Add to this the mounds of frozen snow, and so on, on the roads and the average car gets driven over some very rough terrain. All this jostling around can cause wiring and cable connections to loosen or fall off. This is often the last thing drivers think of when their cars die suddenly. So if you find yourself stranded, check to make sure this isn't the reason. Cars can overheat in the summer for many reasons, but a frequent cause is lack of oil. If you have an oil leak, fix it. Make sure you keep your oil levels up, and change your oil periodically so that it can do its job.

Finally, remember that if you break down in very cold or very hot weather, you'll have to compete for emergency road service with the many other drivers who are in the same situation. It can be a very long wait until you get help, so think twice before you skimp on regular maintenance servicing.

Expressways, Freeways, Thruways, and Beltways

In many ways, expressways, freeways, thruways, parkways, and beltways offer the best of all possible driving worlds. The lanes and shoulders are wide, the roads are well designed and well lit, the signs are easy to see and understand, gas stations and restaurants appear regularly (or signs point to exits where these facilities can be found), and police patrolling the roads will find you if you've had an accident or your car has broken down. Even so, driving on these roads can take some getting used to, especially if most of your driving experience has been in areas where there is little traffic.

Just getting onto some of these roads can be challenging and unnerving. Beltways around major cities in particular are often packed with cars moving at high speeds. Faced with this situation, your natural tendency may be to inch onto the road, but this is not the best way to enter the stream of traffic. Remember, your goal is to merge as smoothly as possible with the other vehicles. You've probably heard that the best way to do this is to accelerate on the entrance ramp and then move quickly onto the highway. That's good advice if traffic is not too bad and the entrance ramp is long enough to give you time to find an opening between oncoming cars. But if the ramp is short or traffic is especially heavy, you may have to slow down or even stop before trying to enter the stream of traffic. In this case, look for an opening, then move quickly onto the highway and accelerate to the speed limit (or, if traffic is moving more slowly, to the speed that the other cars are traveling).

GETTING OFF

On most of these roads, exit signs begin to appear at least one-half of a mile to a mile before the

actual exit. This generally gives you plenty of time to move into the exit lane. Most often the exit lane is the right lane. If the exit is on the left, signs will let you know this well in advance.

Of course, things don't always go as they should. A large truck may be traveling next to you just as you pass the sign indicating that your exit is coming up. With your view blocked, you may be unaware that you are approaching your exit until you're actually there. Or perhaps you saw the sign in plenty of time, but traffic in the exit lane was so packed that you were unable to squeeze in. You may even have been preoccupied with something else and missed your exit entirely. Now what should you do?

First, don't panic. There is a simple solution to all of these situations. If you can't exit safely where you want to or if you've missed your exit, just go on to the next one and turn around. Entrances and exits of an expressway, freeway, or beltway are usually located at the same place but on opposite sides of the highway. Most of the time, as you exit, you'll see a road going over (or under) the expressway. Just follow it. On the other side you'll find the entrance to the expressway going in the opposite direction. Hop on and go back to where you came from. Since you know that the exit you missed is coming up, stay in the exit lane so you'll be in a good position to get off.

THE INTIMIDATION FACTOR

Entering and exiting these roads can be intimidating enough without other drivers driving in ways that may make you feel uncomfortable or bullied. For example, they may tailgate you, flashing their lights for you to go faster or move over despite the fact that you are already driving at the speed limit and there is no opportunity for you to change lanes. If this happens, concentrate on the road ahead and try not to get rattled. The first chance that you get, move over and let them pass. You'll have better luck avoiding impatient drivers like these if you stay out of the fast lane (the lane on the left) unless you are passing another car.

TRUCKS

In terms of intimidation, trucks deserve a special section all of their own. Driving on an expressway with a large truck barreling down the road beside you can make you very nervous. Remember, even though long-distance truckers are skilled drivers, large trucks take much longer to stop than do cars. Instead of slamming on the brakes, a trucker will

react to an obstacle in front of him by trying to change lanes. So try not to drive alongside a truck for any longer than you have to. If the driver has to move into your lane in an emergency, you may get forced off the road or into another lane. It's also very dangerous to pull in front of a truck and then suddenly slow down, as the truck driver may not be able to adjust his speed fast enough to keep from rear-ending you. There's another reason for keeping your distance from a truck, as Sandy and her mother learned.

My mom had just picked me up from soccer practice, and we were coming home on the expressway. The traffic was really heavy, and we got stuck behind this truck that was carrying crates full of something in the back. The driver had his tailgate down, and the crates were sliding back and forth. My mom had just finished saying, "Those boxes are making me very nervous," when one of them fell off the truck right in front of us. There were cars on either side of us and behind us—all going really fast—so she had to drive over the crate. Whatever was in it wrecked the underside of our car. We made it to the side of the road, but that was as far as we got. My mom said she didn't think the truck driver even knew he'd lost some of his load.

Of course, this could have happened on any road, but the chance that it will cause an accident is even greater on a high-speed highway. A good rule of thumb when traveling behind an open truck or a car with anything tied on top is "If it looks like something could fall off, there's a good chance that it will." So do your best to steer clear of these vehicles.

SPEEDING

Traffic on expressways usually moves very quickly. With cars whizzing along on either side of you, it can be easy to find yourself matching their speed and driving much faster than you realize. Regardless of what everyone else seems to be doing, driving 80 miles per hour when the speed limit is 65 is never smart. You are more likely to have a serious accident, and the likelihood that you'll be ticketed increases dramatically.

Speaking of tickets, many drivers think they won't be stopped for speeding if they are going with the flow of traffic, in others words, traveling at the same speed as other cars on the highway. While the police are certainly more likely to target someone who's going much faster than everyone else, that doesn't mean they can't or won't stop you for speeding even if the drivers right next to you are going as fast as you are.

CHANGING LANES

Multilane highways present some additional dangers to watch out for when changing lanes. When moving from the left lane to the middle lane, remember to check the cars in the right lane as well. One of them may be planning to move to the  middle lane too, and you could both end up in the same lane at the same time. Similarly, if you're moving from the right lane to the middle, be aware of the cars in the left lane. And always remember to check your blind spot.

On a road with little traffic, it can be tempting to move across several lanes at a time. Swooping across the road from one side to the other is a very bad idea. Other drivers will not be expecting you to do this and may be accelerating or changing lanes themselves, increasing the chance that the two of you will collide.

TAILGATING

Tailgating, or purposefully driving very close to a car in front of you, is an extremely unsafe thing to do, especially on a high-speed highway. If the driver you are following has to stop suddenly, you're likely to rear-end him. In addition, instead of intimidating the other person (which is what most tailgaters hope to do), you may actually antagonize him, which can spark a road rage incident. Even if all you accomplish is to make him nervous and uncomfortable, this increases the chance that he'll have an accident—one that is likely to involve you as well. Any way you look at it, tailgating is dangerous, so don't do it.

DETOURS

You're happily driving along when all of a sudden detour signs appear. Because of an accident or construction, all cars are being routed off the expressway onto local roads. Great! You picture yourself being dumped on the outskirts of East Podunk without a clue as to how to get where you're going. Before you freak, remember—you aren't the only one in this situation. The highway authorities have probably set up signs or sent traffic officers out to direct all of you.

Most detours are short and clearly marked to help you find your way back to the expressway. Usually the cars in front of you will be driving slowly, so you'll have a chance to find and read the signs. Even if you have difficulty determining where to go, follow the stream of traffic. Most of these drivers are on their way back to the expressway, too. If the cause of the detour is unanticipated, such as an accident, there probably won't be any signs, but traffic officers should be there to direct you. Traffic will usually be going slowly enough that you can stop and ask them for help if you need reassurance that you're headed in the right direction.

DISTANCES BETWEEN EXITS

In heavily populated areas, exits are usually only a mile or two apart. But in less settled places they can be separated by 20 miles or more. So plan ahead when to get gas or take a bathroom break.

TOLLS

Many expressways are toll roads, so be sure to bring enough money to cover the cost. If you plan to use these roads frequently, save yourself time and aggravation by asking your parents to sign up for EZ Pass or whatever automated toll payment system is available in your area.

Cruising Down Country Roads

Country roads... take me home...

Driving in a rural area is very different from driving in a city or the suburbs. If country roads are new to you, being prepared for these differences can help you avoid problems.

ROADS

A major difference is in the roads themselves. Although the main roads in these areas may be four lanes

wide, secondary roads are likely to be much narrower than you are used to, and some may be barely wide enough for two cars. In addition, these roads often have very skimpy shoulders, giving you little or no extra room to move over. Since it can be hard to judge exactly how much space you have, it's a good idea to slow down when passing another car.

Many rural roads, especially in hilly areas, have curves that drastically reduce your ability to see what's ahead. Couple this with wooded areas or crops that may be taller than your car, and visibility can be a real problem. So, even if it looks like there's no one else on the road, take it easy on these little country lanes—you never know what may be around the next bend.

The surfaces of some of these roads may also be different from those you're used to. Although most small country roads are paved, that's not always the case. If all of your driving experience has been on asphalt, you may be in for a surprise the first time you try to make a sharp turn or sudden stop on gravel or dirt. These surfaces don't provide the same traction as asphalt, and you can skid off the road if you're not careful.

Finding your way around in the country may also be more difficult for you. Street signs and signs indicating nearby towns are usually fewer, smaller, and much easier to miss than those in the city and suburbs. Even if you can find people to ask, you may have trouble following their directions. For example, being told to turn at the old barn, keep going until you reach an alfalfa field, and turn right a mile after that may not be of much help if all the barns in the area look old to you and you don't have a clue what alfalfa is. So, if possible, it's a good idea to carry a map of the area with you. Maps of most areas can be found online, so you may want to give that a try before setting out.

LIGHTING

Driving in rural areas at night can be a nerve-racking experience if you are used to well-lit city or suburban roads. Secondary country roads are DARK! There are generally no streetlights, and even intersections are often unlit. Being unable to read signs or recognize landmarks can make you feel like you're lost, even if

you aren't. Using your bright lights can help you get a better sense of your surroundings, but be sure to lower them when oncoming traffic approaches. And if you have to drive at night, check first to be sure you know where you're going.

FILL HER UP

Even if you plan to stick to the major roads, there are one or two things you should keep in mind. Granted, these roads are likely to be better lit; have passing lanes, decent-sized shoulders, and more visible signs; and go through settled areas. In fact, they may not be much different from the ones you're used to. But you may not notice how few and far between the gas stations are until you need one. Waiting until your gas gauge is close to empty before refilling the tank is OK in the suburbs, where gas stations are easy to find, but it can be a big mistake in a rural area. Try to keep your gas tank half-full when driving in the country, at least until you have a good idea where the gas stations are.

As in urban and suburban places, many gas stations in rural areas accept credit cards at the tanks, so in that sense they're likely to be open at night.

But that's probably all that will be open, particularly if you are somewhat off the beaten path. Small and even medium-sized towns in rural areas tend to close down early, and in many parts of the country, little except churches are open on Sunday. So keep this in mind and plan ahead.

ANIMALS

A very important difference between country driving and driving in the city or suburbs is the chance of encountering wildlife. While it can be exciting to glimpse a fox, an owl, or some other animal you've always wanted to see, wildlife can also pose a significant threat to you. The animals that present the greatest risk are deer. Despite almost 100 years of co-existing with automobiles, deer have yet to learn that it's unwise to bolt in front of a car. Hitting a deer is not only upsetting but dangerous. Deer are heavy, and a collision with one can cause serious damage to your car. Worse, many people are injured or killed each year in accidents involving deer. So, for your own safety, as well as theirs, keep the following tips in mind.

The likelihood of hitting a deer increases dramatically in the fall. During this period deer are preoccupied with mating and are even less likely to be paying attention to you. Regardless of the time of year, deer are most active shortly after dawn and at twilight—precisely when it may be hardest for you to see them. And as Eric and his girlfriend learned, it pays to remember that where there's one deer, there are likely to be two or more.

We were driving through the Blue Ridge Mountains, just taking in the fall foliage, when suddenly a deer ran across the road in front of us. She was absolutely beautiful! We were so busy watching her bound into the woods that we almost didn't notice a second deer that was right behind her. I swerved to miss it and plowed into a tree. We were okay, and so was the deer, but the whole front of the car was totaled.

Hitting one of the many other animals that can be on the road—such as dogs, cats, raccoons, opposums, skunks, and foxes—may not pose the same danger to you, but it can be equally upsetting. Remember, just because an animal is walking or sitting on the side of the road doesn't mean it will stay there. It is impossible to predict when one of these creatures may suddenly dart in front of you, so slow down and be ready to stop when you see them.

SPEED ZONES

On both primary and secondary rural roads, the speed limit often drops quickly from 55 or 60 miles an hour to 35 miles as you approach a town. Don't think that slowing down to 45 or 50 for the minute and a half that it takes you to go through the town is enough. Rural towns (and their local police) take these speed limits very seriously.

Big City Lights

Just the idea of driving through highly congested cities such as New York, Chicago, or Washington makes many people from suburban or rural areas nervous. But while it's true that city driving presents some challenges, with a little preparation, you can survive—and even enjoy—the experience.

TOLLS

Some cities may have tolls on certain roads or bridges, either as you enter or exit town or within the city itself. For starters, find out ahead of time whether this is true of the city where you're going, or better yet, be sure

to have some extra cash on hand. Many toll booths now accept EZ Pass or a similar automated payment system. Be careful not to get in a lane for automated payment if you don't have an automated pass. In some places, this can result in a fine.

FINDING YOUR WAY AROUND

By far the biggest difficulty you're likely to face is finding your way around. Urban road signs can be

very confusing, often making sense only to the people who live there. Not only may available information be unclear, but there is generally very little time for you to make decisions. In the suburbs or the country, you may be able to slow down or pull over to figure out which direction to go, but this usually isn't feasible in a city. As a result, you may find yourself being swept down the street in a stream of traffic, trying to decide in the next three seconds what to do at the intersection.

Fortunately, this is one situation where a little advance planning goes a very long way. Before arriving in a city, get a street map and plan your route. (Again, the Internet is a good source of maps.) Assume that you will encounter glitches—like forgetting the directions—and be prepared to deal with them. For example, since trying to read a map while driving is a very bad idea, write the route on a piece of paper in large, easy-to-read letters beforehand, and keep it within reach. Then if you forget where you're supposed to go, you can take a quick look at your directions. Even better, try to have a friend along to be your navigator.

Another common snag to prepare for is the presence of one-way streets. Since maps often don't indicate which streets are one-way only, you may find that you can't use the route you've so carefully worked out because a street you planned to take goes in the wrong direction. Don't panic! Most cities alternate the direction of their one-way streets, so the next street will usually be going in the direction you want.

In addition to figuring out how to get to your destination, study the map to see how the city is organized. Some cities were designed according to a plan—knowing what that plan is can be a big help if you get lost. For example, Washington, D.C., is divided into four quadrants: Northeast, Northwest, Southeast, and Southwest. If you're trying to get to M Street NW, and the sign in front of you says Rhode Island Avenue NE, you know that you're on the wrong side of the city and need to head west. If your car has a compass, it's easy to figure out which way is west. If not, just stop and ask someone.

Other clues to the underlying plan may not be on your map, but can be figured out if you are observant. If you keep your eyes open in downtown New York, for example, you'll notice that the even-numbered streets are one-way going east, while the odd-numbered streets are one-way going west.

If you get lost, don't be afraid to ask for directions. Most folks will be happy to help you if they can. Just remember to find a well-lit place where there are a number of people before you pull over to ask.

Finally, it's always possible that something unexpected will throw you off track. That's when a cell phone can be a lifesaver, as Julie discovered.

I'd driven from Long Island into Manhattan a couple of times before with no problem. The expressway runs right into the Midtown Tunnel, so all I have to do to get home from Manhattan is to remember where the entrance to the tunnel is. That day, I'd gone into the city with a friend, and we were on our way home. But when we got to the tunnel, the police had closed it down for some emergency. Traffic was jammed up everywhere, and one of the cops said our best bet to get to Long Island was to take the Williamsburg Bridge. He gave us directions to the bridge but didn't mention that it goes to Brooklyn, which is nowhere near the expressway. I'd never been to Brooklyn in my whole life. We got so lost it wasn't funny! The people we asked for directions only knew how to go by subway, which didn't do us any good. Finally, some guy tried to tell us how to get on the BQE, but we had no idea what that was. It was getting late and we were really starting to get scared! Luckily, my friend was able to get a hold of her uncle who lived in Manhattan. He tried to give us directions over the phone, but by then it was dark and we were too terrified to leave the gas station we'd pulled into, so he had to get in his car, drive to Brooklyn, and lead us to the expressway.

Julie thinks things might have been different if she'd taken a map along, as her mother suggested.

At least then, I'd have seen that the BQE was another expressway and that I could have taken it straight from the bridge to where it hooks up with the road I wanted.

SAFETY

In addition to knowing your route, you'll need to take a few extra safety precautions when driving in a city. In general, it's a good idea to lock your doors and keep your windows closed or only slightly cracked at the top, particularly when driving in slow or stop-and-go traffic. The reason is simple— while you're stuck in a traf-

fic jam, a pedestrian can easily open your unlocked door or stick a hand through your window

and grab your camera, laptop, backpack, or other valuable item. While the thief runs down the street, you're trapped in traffic, unable to drive after him or leave your car to chase him. Even more important, while the chance that you will be a victim of a carjacking is *very* remote, locking your door and keeping your windows up helps to ensure this never happens to you. You should also *always* lock any tempting items in your trunk rather than keeping them in full view in the backseat. Even while you're driving, you should keep your pocketbook or backpack under a seat. There's no need to advertise that you have something worth stealing.

THE URBAN OBSTACLE COURSE

For many people from rural or suburban areas, the second most difficult thing about driving in a city is negotiating a path through the urban obstacle course. Although cities vary greatly, drivers in some places may find themselves dodging giant

potholes, jaywalking pedestrians, double-parked cars, careening taxicabs, and bike messengers who seem bent on suicide. As if you didn't have enough to think about already, you'll need to keep an eye out for these obstacles as well.

STAYING CALM

It's easy to get rattled when you think you might be lost, just missed being sideswiped, or have a pack of impatient drivers be-hind you honking away. Since it's even harder to drive when you're nervous, the first step in dealing with these situations is to calm down. Take a deep breath and concentrate on what you're doing and where you're going. If you really feel like you're losing it, try to find a place to pull over for a minute. Remember, people who aren't as bright as you drive through the city every day—you can do it too, if you just relax.

With limited parking, many cities are very aggressive about enforcing their parking laws. You risk a hefty fine for parking in an illegal space, and in some places your car will actually be towed. This is not something you want to happen to you! In addition to being inconvenient and time-consuming, getting your car back can be very expensive. On top of the parking ticket, you will have to pay a significant towing charge, as well as the cost of transportation to get you to the out-of-the-way place where your car is being stored.

To avoid this, be sure to read parking signs carefully. Some cities are notorious for their unusual or confusing parking restrictions; so if it's unclear whether or not a particular spot is OK, find a place somewhere else. Also, be prepared to have to pay for parking, either at a parking meter or in a commercial garage. Although free street parking will be available in many parts of the city, paid parking is often the only option in the most congested areas. Some parking meters now accept credit cards, but you'll need quarters for most meters, so be sure to bring a supply with you. In addition, all of the spots on the street will require you to parallel park, so if you haven't done it in a while, you might want to practice a little at home. Finally, parking garages are expensive, but they offer some advantages. For example, you don't have to run back every hour to feed a meter or struggle to squeeze into a tiny parking spot while other drivers honk at you. Some people also feel their car is safer in a garage. But keep in mind that parking garages do not accept responsibility for items left in an unlocked car, so put all valuable items in your trunk and lock it.

GETTING GAS

Oddly, driving in the city has one thing in common with driving in rural areas—gas stations may be in short supply. With the streets of most cities crowded with cars, you would think that there would be a service station on every corner. However, developers are generally reluctant to use valuable real estate for a few gas tanks when they could put up a more profitable high-rise office building instead. As a result, gas stations are likely to be located on the edge of town, in more industrial areas, or near truck routes, expressways, and beltways. To be safe, it's best to fill up before you enter the city It's usually cheaper as well. If you'll be staying for a few days, find out as soon as possible where the nearest gas station is.

When It's Not Your Car

There can be any number of reasons why you may find yourself driving a car that you're unfamiliar with. You may have borrowed a friend's car because yours is being repaired. You may need a bigger car to carry a large load. Or maybe you didn't plan to drive at all, but the person you were with had too much to drink, so you took over the wheel. Before you take off down the road, however, there are a few things you should do first.

ANY CAR THAT'S NOT YOURS

The first thing is to remember is to adjust the mirrors and the seat to fit you. Then take a look at where the knobs and switches are placed on the dashboard. You don't want to be fumbling around later while you're on the road, trying to figure out how to turn on the air conditioner or close 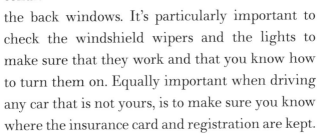 the back windows. It's particularly important to check the windshield wipers and the lights to make sure that they work and that you know how to turn them on. Equally important when driving any car that is not yours, is to make sure you know where the insurance card and registration are kept.

A FRIEND'S CAR

Although your parents probably keep their car in good condition, the same may not be true of your friends. The younger you are, the more likely it is that your friends have older cars and perhaps have skimped a little (or maybe a lot) on regular maintenance. In other words, the car you're about to borrow may be a serious clunker. People often get so used to their own car's quirks that they can

Whoa! You'll need the emergency brake!

forget to mention them—like the car leaks transmission fluid and it needs to be replaced every day. To avoid unpleasant surprises, ask your friend if there is anything special you should know about the car *before* you take off. Amber found this out the hard way.

My roommate and I borrowed her boyfriend's pickup truck to move from our old apartment to our new place. There we were, halfway in between with everything we owned crammed in the back, and the truck just died. It was three o'clock on a Friday afternoon in the summer, and the temperature was in the mid-nineties. We almost sweltered to death waiting for the highway emergency service to show up. Turned out that we were out of gas. We couldn't believe it! The gas gauge still said half full. When we finally got to a phone and called her boyfriend, he said, "Oh, yeah . . . I forgot to tell you. The gas gauge doesn't register below half full. You have to keep track of how many miles you've driven since the last time you filled her up." We could have killed him!

A MANUAL CAR

Of course, you won't try to borrow a car with a manual transmission if you have no idea at all of how to shift gears with a clutch. But even if you've had some experience with these cars, there may be a few things you've forgotten if you haven't driven one in a while. Putting on the emergency break may be one of them.

Jenny was very pleased with herself when she managed to drive her cousin's car across town and back without a problem.

He'd just had it repainted. I knew he'd be furious if anything happened to his precious paint job, so I was supercareful. His house is up a really steep driveway. I was so happy to get the car back to him without a scratch that I just put the thing in neutral, grabbed the keys, and hopped out.

Her cousin was standing in the front yard at the time, so he had a clear view of his car as it rolled back down the driveway and smashed into a car parked across the street.

I forgot that you have to put the emergency brake on with a manual car. My car's an automatic, and you don't have to do this.

A SPORT-UTILITY VEHICLE

The first thing you'll notice when driving an SUV is that the center of gravity is much higher than in a regular car. As a result, it is more likely to tip over  if you turn abruptly. It also takes longer to stop one of these vehicles. So in addition to turning more carefully, be sure to leave more room between you and the car in front of you in case you need to brake suddenly.

Newer SUVs and other high-end cars can be so loaded with accessories, gadgets, and instruments that the dashboard can look more like an airplane cockpit. While you should familiarize yourself with the controls of any car you haven't driven before, this is especially true of more expensive, recent models. Mike discovered this the hard way.

My uncle lent me his new SUV for the weekend so a friend and I could go camping upstate. Before we even got there, it started pouring down rain. I figured out how to turn on the windshield wipers, but neither one of us could find a way to

**close the windows. We rode for twenty minutes, holding our
jackets up to keep the water out, before we finally found a gas
station where the guy knew how to do it.**

Visibility from certain angles may also be restricted in newer SUVs. Because of the height of
an SUV, the view from the front is better than in
most cars. However, some of the more upscale
versions of these vehicles have TV screens hanging down in the back that cut down significantly
on your ability to use the rearview mirror. You
should adjust the mirrors anytime you drive a car
that's not yours, but this may require some real
fine-tuning in an SUV with these accessories.

INSURANCE ISSUES

Any tickets that you get as the driver of a car,
whether it is your car or not, will go on your
record and can cause your (or your parents') insurance rates to go
up. But assum-
ing you have
the owner's
permission
to borrow
a car, his
or her insurance will cover you if you have an
accident. This doesn't mean that you will be completely off the hook however. The owner's insur-

ance company may then try to recoup the money they've paid out by making a claim against your insurance company.

This also means that you should think carefully before you let another person drive your car. If your friend has an accident in your car, your insurance will have to pay for any injuries and property damage, and your rates will probably increase significantly.

TO BORROW OR NOT TO BORROW

Unless it's an emergency, it's sometimes better not to borrow a car at all than to borrow one that is likely to break down or is unsafe to drive. If you suspect that the car you're borrowing is a real lemon, you might want to consider other forms of transportation.

On another note, if you know or suspect that the owner of the car smokes dope or uses drugs,

think twice before you borrow his or her car. At the very least, you'll want to be sure this person has not left drugs under the seat, stashed in the glove compartment, or hidden somewhere else. If you get stopped for some reason and the police find drugs, they are unlikely to believe you when you claim, "It's not mine! I have no idea how it got there!" Better yet, protect yourself and find another car to borrow.

Driving with Children or Pets

Driving with children or pets presents some special challenges. Since some of the tips for driving with pets also apply to children, let's deal with pets first.

PETS

Leaving Your Pet in the Car
Never leave an animal in a closed car in the heat *even if the window is cracked*, as it can die within a few minutes. When deciding if it's OK to leave your pet, remember that temperatures outside the

car can be deceiving—the inside of a car is likely to be much hotter. With its heavy coat and inability to sweat, your pet will have a harder time in the heat than you; so if you think it's getting too warm for you, it's definitely too hot for a dog or cat. Although it may not be particularly hot outside, if the car is parked in the sun, the animal can still overheat and die. And remember, a car left in the shade may be in full sun when you come back.

Open Windows

Do not open your car windows wide enough for your pet to jump, squeeze, or wriggle out. Regardless of how much your dog loves riding with his head out the window or how well behaved he's been in the past, something  unexpected may catch his eye and prompt him to leap out of the car. This is especially true if you are driving slowly.

Restraints

Consider keeping small or active pets restrained while you're driving. There are seat belts made especially for pets that you can buy if you wish.

Smaller animals can be placed in a carrier with a regular seat belt fastened through the handle. If you have a larger dog, you may already have a crate that the animal can ride in. Restraining your pet will not only help you focus on the road but will also keep the animal from being hurt if you have to make an abrupt stop. And it also helps to prevent unexpected escapes when you open the door.

CHILDREN

Seat Belts

All children should be restrained in an age-appropriate seat belt or safety seat. Always, always, always! Never take more children than you have seat belts for. It's just not worth the risk. If the child is going to be riding in a car seat, make sure the child's parent installs it properly. If it's not used in the right way, a car seat can be dangerous. Also, remember that it's very unsafe to let small children ride in the front seat, whether they are in a car seat or not. If the air bag deploys, it can injure or kill the child.

Windows and Doors

Make sure that the doors are locked, since children may open them while you are driving, and fall out. You'll also want to keep the back windows closed. Kids love to wave action figures, dolls, and other toys out the window. Naturally, a number of these end up sailing out the window onto the highway. The child will be upset over losing a toy, and a flying object is dangerous to other drivers. Many cars have special child-safety locks or other locks for the windows and doors that only the driver controls. Check your manual to see where they are located, and use them when traveling with young children.

Leaving Kids in the Car

Leaving children in a car is a very dangerous thing to do. Like pets, they can suffer heatstroke if left in a car on a hot day. Unlike pets, they also have an amazing ability to open windows or doors you thought were secure, play with the cigarette lighter, or put the car in gear. In addition, there is always the chance that someone will steal your car, even with a child in it. In fact, the child may be the primary target. Leaving a child in a car in a large parking lot is especially risky. There have been a number of cases in which cars containing children have been stolen and the kids—some of them infants—dumped on the side of a highway miles away. In other cases, parents have returned to find their car there but their child gone. Don't take the chance of this happening to you.

Distractions

Children can be extremely distracting. Even one child trying to tell you about his day can make it hard for you to concentrate if you're trying to figure out where to go next or how to make your way through traffic. Focusing on your driving can be even more difficult when you have several

children in the car. Excited voices can become shrieks, joking around can turn into fights or tears, and just the presence of squirming kids in the backseat can take your mind off the road. If you're having trouble concentrating, pull over for a minute so you and the kids can calm down. And if you find that driving with more than one child is too much, don't do it.

Dealing with Your Parents

Like many things in your life, your ability to drive can become just one more thing to fight over with your parents. Before you get involved in a major struggle with them, take the time to prepare for some of these issues.

NEGOTIATING DRIVING PRIVILEGES

Regardless of your age, if you're driving your parents' car or you're on their insurance policy, they have the final control over how and when

you use the car. To head off problems or fights, you
and your par-
ents should sit
down together
and establish
clear-cut rules for using the car, including the
consequences of not following them. Many fami-
lies find it helpful to write these rules down in a
contract.

Some of the issues you may want to discuss include what happens if you don't bring the car
home at the agreed upon time; whether you have
permission to let a friend or someone else drive
the car and, if so, under what circumstances; who
pays for gas; who pays for regular servicing if
your parents have given you a car; and who pays
for any increase in your parents' insurance premium resulting from traffic tickets you may get.
If you're going to be sharing a car with other
family members, you should also discuss when
and how often you'll get to use the car. Finally,
you'll want to have a clear understanding of the
things that will make your parents take away or
limit your driving privileges.

BEING CONSIDERATE

In addition to following the rules you and your
parents have established, they'll expect you to be

considerate of others who use the car.

In Jake's case, forgetting to do this landed him in big trouble.

It was already past the time I was supposed to be home and I didn't want to make myself even later by stopping for gas. When I put the car in the garage, the needle was on empty; but there was enough there to get to the gas station, so I didn't think it was a big deal.

Unfortunately, Jake's mother thought it was a very big deal. Never dreaming that he would use up all the gas and not replace it, she hopped in the car the next morning and drove off to work. It didn't occur to her to check the gas gauge until the car sputtered to a halt on the freeway.

She was so ticked off that it was months before she let me use the car again.

One of the disadvantages of getting your license is that you may now be expected to pick your little brother up from baseball practice, run errands for your mother, or take on other responsibilities that you weren't able to do before you could drive. While this can be a bummer, it's part of the deal—so you should try to do these things as graciously as possible.

DRIVING WITH YOUR PARENTS

Having one of your parents in the passenger seat while you're at the wheel may be the quickest way to make nervous wrecks out of both of you. Shauna has had an especially hard time with this.

> I hate it! My mom's not so bad, but my father's impossible! He makes me so nervous I can hardly think, and then I make mistakes I never make when I'm by myself. Even when he's not criticizing me—which is almost never—I can feel him twitching in his seat, just waiting for the ride to end. Once he got me so upset that I started crying and had to pull over.

The truth is that no matter how calm they may seem, most parents are terrified by the fact that their children are now driving—some are just better at hiding it than others. Often their fear has little to do with you

or how well they think you drive. It's just that, as drivers, they know from experience how easily a disastrous accident resulting in crippling injury or death can occur, and they are tortured by the idea that you might be hurt or might hurt others. For parents who are really worried, the tiniest mistake—actual or imagined—that you make while driving seems like evidence that their worst fears will come true. Of course, this becomes a self-fulfilling prophecy—the more nervous they are, the more nervous you become and the more likely you are to do something wrong.

For this reason it's sometimes not a good idea for parents to try to teach their own children to drive. When you're first learning, you're bound to make mistakes—sometimes big ones—and it's better to have an instructor who can respond calmly when this happens. After you get your license, you should expect that both you and your parents will be a little tense when they first ride with you. As time goes by without any major incidents, they'll become more comfortable with your driving and you'll be less easily rattled by their presence.

In rare cases like Shauna's, however, it may be a good idea for both parties to agree not to ride together for a while. If you're in a situation like this and your parents continue to have serious concerns about your driving ability, perhaps they should talk to your driver's ed teacher or another adult who's ridden with you to get a more objective opinion of how you're doing. Of course, there's always the outside chance that you really do need further help, but preferably not from them. If so, you might consider signing up for a brushup course with a professional driving instructor.

CHAPTER 13

Pressures, Pressures, Pressures

MAINTAINING YOUR COOL WITH FRIENDS

Like many other things in your life, being able to drive comes with its own set of peer pressures. Wanting to be like everyone else may be the cause of some of these pressures. Other pressures may result from feeling that you should do what your friends ask. How you handle these pressures will be a big factor in how much you enjoy driving, as well as how safe you're likely to be behind the wheel.

BEING THE FIRST OR
LAST TO DRIVE

Everyone else you know can jump in a car and just take off. But you're still dependent on your parents or public transportation to get around. Whether you haven't gotten your license yet or you just don't have access to a car, chances are you feel tied down and decidedly uncool. Josh described the feeling this way:

> It wasn't just that I didn't have my license or a car, because some of my friends didn't either. But they could always ride to school with someone in our group. I lived too far out of town for anyone to drive out, pick me up, and get to school on time. So there I was at seventeen—still riding the school bus. I felt like a total loser.

Although being the last among your friends to drive is a drag, being the first isn't always so great either. Claire was the first in her crowd to get her license and her parents gave her a car to go with it.

At first, it was great! We'd all hop in my car and hit the mall, go to the movies, whatever. But after a while, I began to feel like a taxi service. People were calling me to take them places I didn't even want to go. It got really bad when friends of mine started dating each other. We'd all go somewhere in my car, and when we got there, they'd pair off and just leave me hanging. To see what would happen, I told them my mom needed to borrow my car for a while 'cause hers died. After that, they pretty much stopped including me, and that hurt!

The thing to remember about problems like these is that they tend to disappear after a while. In a year or so, everyone in a group of friends will usually be able to drive, so no one will get stuck being a chauffeur. And with time those—like Josh—who haven't had access to a car may be able to earn enough money to buy a used one.

STATUS ISSUES

In addition to being a means of transportation, cars are also a status symbol. In some crowds, just

having one raises your standing. In others, everyone has a car and what's important is what kind and how new it is. It can be hard if you don't have a car or if you feel that yours isn't "right."

Of course, there may be ways that you can change this situation. But first, ask yourself why it matters so much. It's one thing if not having a car keeps you from doing activities that are important to you, such as playing on a sports team or working on the school newspaper. In this case, having a car would probably improve your life. But it's another thing to believe that you'd finally be popular if you just had some really great wheels. If this is the case, you might want to rethink why you're trying to impress people who are more interested in your car than they are in you.

STUPID GAMES, ONE-UPMANSHIP, AND DOING THINGS YOU KNOW ARE DUMB

One of the biggest challenges most new drivers face is being pressured by others to do things that are danger-ous. Since many of your friends may not have their licenses or access to a car, if you have both, you're likely to get a lot of pressure to pack as many passengers in your car as you can. This may not seem like such a big deal. But with six people in the backseat, the only thing you'll be able to see in your rearview mirror is a line of heads. And those four other people squeezed in the front with you will make it very difficult for you to move, much less drive the car safely. In addition, if you're carrying too many people, you won't have enough seat belts, risking serious injury to you and your passengers and jeopardizing your insurance coverage.

Even just fooling around with others can turn into a competitive situation in which you may feel your reputation is somehow at stake. A good example of this is when a friend passes you on the road and makes a joking remark about your car being too old to catch up with him. As he disappears in a cloud of dust, you have two choices. You can take his challenge as a joke and laugh, or you can decide to show him he's wrong and tear down the road after him. Unfortunately, what starts out as a game of one-upmanship between friends can turn into a deadly accident or escalate into a not-so-friendly confrontation before either of you realizes what's happening. No one's reputation is worth that.

In other cases, you may be pressured to do things that are clearly illegal, dangerous, or both—like picking up a couple of six-packs to tide you and your friends over until you get to the party. Most of the time, you already know that these are bad ideas—what you may not know is how to refuse without looking uncool.

In handling these situations, keep in mind that people will often try to pressure you to do something that they wouldn't do if they were in your place. After all, it's not their license that may be revoked if you're caught speeding or driving while intoxicated. If you think they wouldn't take the risk themselves, remind them of that. Sometimes a simple response, such as, "Yeah, like you'd ever do that if it meant losing *your* license," ends the discussion.

Andre has another strategy for maintaining his image while refusing to do something dangerous or illegal. "I just say, 'No way, man! I don't need any more hassles with the cops than I already have.'" In reality, Andre's driving record is spotless and the cops have no idea he even exists. But saying this gives the impression that he isn't afraid to take chances and does risky things all the time. "It's kind of a lie," he admitted. "But it works."

Rachelle reminds herself that she's the one in the position of power. This makes it easier for her to stand up to pressures from others. She has the following advice:

Remember, you're the one with the car, so you're the cool one. They're the ones bumming a ride from you, so they're the uncool ones. You know it and they know it, so *act* like it!

I had a friend who thought it was cute to keep turning on my flashers while I was trying to drive. I told him to cut it out, and he just said, "What's with you?" and did it again. So I pulled over to the curb and said, "Knock it off or get out of the car right now." I guess he thought he'd look pretty stupid walking home, so he stopped.

Unfortunately, there are always some people who just won't quit. They keep up the pressure, acting as if you're a wimp or a nerd for not doing what they want. The question here is, Just how much does their opinion matter to you? Enough to have your driving privileges restricted? Enough to lose your license? Or even enough to risk your life? Probably not, if you think about it. And if refusing to do something you don't want to do would hurt your friendship, are these people really your friends in the first place? Again, probably not. In cases like these, the only response that works is no. You don't need to justify why you're refusing— the fact that you think it's a bad idea is reason enough. If they can't accept this, forget them. You deserve better friends.

When You Are a Passenger

You know from your own experience as a driver that your passengers can make it either easier or harder for you to drive. But you may not have given much thought to how you rate as a passenger yourself. Do drivers look forward to having you in the car, or can they hardly wait to unload you? Anything that makes your time in the car safer is a good idea, so you'll want to do what you can to be a good passenger.

DISTRACTING BEHAVIOR

Distractions are a major cause of accidents, especially those involving young drivers. No one is suggesting that you sit mute and motionless for the whole ride, but you'll certainly want to avoid doing things that are guaranteed to be distracting. Having a heated argument with the driver is one of them. This is not the time to have that knock-down-drag-out battle with your boyfriend or girlfriend about a serious problem in your relationship. While the driver is screaming at you, he or she is probably not watching the road. And even if the driver manages to keep his eyes focused on the traffic, you can be sure that's not where his mind is.

Getting along a little too well can be just as much of a problem. While it may seem like a hot thing to do, snuggling, kissing, or fondling the driver are sure to distract him or her and are best postponed until the motor is turned off. Even less intense things that you normally do with friends—such as joking around, sharing the latest gossip, or debating which CD to listen to—can make it harder for a driver to pay attention to the road.

PRESSURING THE DRIVER

Pressuring the driver to do something unsafe or something he's uncomfortable with is more than distracting—it's downright stupid. So what if he could legally go a little faster if it means he's less in control of the car? And it doesn't matter if you think he has plenty of room to pass the car in front of him, it matters what *he* thinks. He's the one who's going to have to pull it off. If someone is a little more cautious than you would be in the same situation, give him a break. He knows his own limitations and deserves credit for not trying to do something he's not sure he can handle.

HELPFUL THINGS YOU CAN DO

There are several things you can do that will make it easier for the driver. If your job is to be the navigator, keep the map or directions handy so you don't have to fumble around for them at the last minute. When it comes time to tell the driver what to do, be sure you are clear. For example, frantically yelling "Turn here!" a few feet before an intersection is not particularly helpful. It leaves the poor driver wondering, "Turn where?!!" or "Right or left?!!" Instead of making the driver swerve across two lanes of traffic in an effort to go where you're pointing, give her a fighting chance with clear, specific directions, such as, "You're going to be making a right turn at the next light."

You can also take charge of changing the radio station and loading the CD player. And most important, while the car is moving, you should be the one who makes or answers any phone calls, whether it's on your cell phone or hers. If you don't know how to work her phone, ask her to show you before you start out.

Trying to eat or drink while driving is not a good idea. Nothing is more likely to take a driver's mind off driving than a steaming cup of coffee spilled in her lap. And even if she manages not to spill anything, eating or drinking leaves her with only one hand available for driving.

However, if the driver insists on doing this, offer to hold her food or drink.

Finally, being a good passenger also means taking responsibility for your own safety. Always buckle your seat belt, even if the driver or other passengers don't. If the driver is doing things that are clearly unsafe— such as driving recklessly, at high speeds, or while intoxicated— and you can't convince him to stop and let you drive, then you need to get out of the car fast. (For tips on how to do this, see chapter 16.)

Road Rage

Unfortunately, the car has become the great equalizer. When protected by a shell of metal, even ordinarily timid people may begin to see themselves as the Terminator. Driving a car gives many people a feeling of increased power and invulnerability. In addition, with a quick get-away made possible by a car, some drivers are less concerned about getting caught. As a result, many drivers think they can use their cars as an easy way of expressing anger and frustration. Better known as road rage, this behavior can end in serious injury or death. You do not want to become a sad statistic.

CONTROLLING YOUR ANGER

It's only natural to be annoyed when someone cuts in front of you, causing you to slam on your brakes; steals the parking spot you were getting ready to back into; or curses you out for not moving out of the way. And it can be very tempting to let this person know exactly what you think of him, or to retaliate in some way. However, there are several excellent reasons not to do so: (1) Believe it or not, striking back probably won't make you feel any better. If anything, it's likely to get you even more worked up. (2) It probably won't make the person in question feel embarrassed, stupid, or sorry, nor will it make him more likely to apologize. In fact, he may be hoping for a fight, and you certainly don't want to give him the pleasure of pushing you into one. (3) Most importantly, it's impossible to predict what the person you're yelling at will do in response. Too many people have gotten into verbal battles only to find things escalating out of control when the other person pulls out a tire iron or a gun. As Derek learned, even a relatively mild reaction can get you in real trouble.

My girlfriend and I were crossing an intersection. We had the light when this guy almost ran us over. I slammed my hand down on his fender—not enough to dent it or anything—and said, "Watch where you're going!" As I was walking away, he jumped out of the car and slugged me from behind. I was down on the ground with him kicking me in the head before I even knew what happened. I'm not a wimp, but this guy was huge! All I could do was to curl up in a ball and try to protect myself. A cabdriver and some other pedestrians tried to pull him off. But the thing that finally got him to stop was when my girlfriend screamed that she had called the police and given them his license number. When he heard that, he got back in his car and drove off. I had to go to the hospital and have an MRI on my head and neck. I didn't have any permanent injuries, but I was furious for weeks.

Tom has been a high-school driver's ed instructor for years, and he knows just how easy it is to get sucked into a bad situation when you let your temper get the best of you. His advice for dealing with any potential confrontation is: "Think! Then think again. Respect yourself, respect your car, and respect other drivers (even if they don't act like they deserve it)."

PARKING SPACES

Surprisingly, some of the worst confrontations are over parking spaces. In many cities parking on the street is so limited that fights may break out between drivers competing for an empty space. Even at a crowded mall it's not uncommon to see two drivers arguing over a parking spot. It's certainly easy to become impatient or lose your temper when you've been circling for twenty minutes trying to find a place to put your car. But getting into a fight about a parking space just isn't worth it. You risk getting hurt, and the other person may take his hostility out on your car. Remember, after you've parked your car and left, it will be unprotected. Once you're gone, the person you angered may return and let the air out of your tires, break your side mirrors, or gouge your doors with something sharp.

DEALING WITH SOMEONE ELSE'S ROAD RAGE

Usually you can head off a fight if you don't respond to another driver's aggressive or confronta-

tional behavior. On rare occasions, however, someone may be determined to harass you, perhaps by trying to force you off the road or by pulling in front of you, then slowing down and not letting you pass. At the bare minimum, this is likely to be a scary or frustrating experience; at worst, it may cause you to have an accident.

If you have a cell phone, now is the time to use it. Call the police immediately, explain what is happening to you, and give them your location and the license-plate number of the other car. Follow their instructions until they reach you. If you don't have a cell phone, drive to a convenience store or a restaurant and ask someone to call the police for you. Stay inside the store until the police arrive. Even if the person follows you in there, he's less likely to hassle you with other people around. Of course, if there's a police station nearby and you know how to get there, this is an even better place to go.

Finally, you'll want the time you spend driving to be a safe and pleasant experience. There's nothing fun about screaming your lungs out at

someone else, having your car damaged, or getting into a fight in which you or someone else
gets hurt. So do your best to avoid road rage.
Don't start a fight, and don't let yourself get
sucked into one.

Alcohol, Illegal Drugs, and Sedating Medications

By now, you've been warned many times about the dangers of drinking and driving, and you already know that the biggest risk you can take behind the wheel is to mix the two. But unfortunately, your own drinking isn't the only thing you need to be concerned about. Even if you're not drinking, you can be killed or seriously injured by someone else who is driving drunk. Three out of every ten Americans will be involved at some time in an alcohol-related accident. These accidents are particularly deadly, accounting for over 40 percent of fatal crashes. Obviously, you'll want to do everything possible to avoid becoming one of these statistics.

Alcohol poses other dangers as well. Besides affecting your driving ability, alcohol can also affect your judgment. Many minor confrontations that ordinarily would be laughed off or ignored can spark deadly cases of road rage when fueled by alcohol. Being able to deal successfully with the many issues related to alcohol will play a big part in your becoming a good driver.

TO DRINK OR NOT TO DRINK

Although you may not be able to influence what others do, you certainly have control over your own decisions. One thing is clear—if you're not of legal drinking age, you shouldn't even consider drinking, much less drinking and driving. Assuming that you manage not to injure or kill someone (which is a big assumption), being caught even once driving and drinking while underage will have long-term consequences for your license and insurance, to say nothing of your parents' willingness to let you use the car. Even if you are old enough, if your drinking causes an accident in which a friend dies or you are paralyzed, nothing—including the best medical care, the most money, or the deepest remorse—will be able to bring that person back or enable you to walk again.

Sara and Kendra learned this lesson the hard way at a party in their senior year.

> We ran out of soda, and the girl giving the party asked us to run to the store and get some more. We'd both had a few drinks, but no way were we drunk. I didn't feel like driving, so we took Kendra's car. We never even got to the store. A van rammed into us on the passenger's side, where I was sitting. Kendra got bruised pretty badly, but I had cuts all over my face and my leg was crushed. For a while, it looked like they might even have to amputate it, so I guess I was lucky in a way.

Sara doesn't blame Kendra.

> It was really the other guy's fault. And it could just as easily have been me who was driving as her.

But sadly, the accident caused Sara and Kendra to drift apart.

> She was my best friend, but she felt guilty, and that made it hard for her to hang out with me. And I was angry at her for a long time. The thing was that she could go on with her life like nothing happened, but I can't. I have a big scar on my face,

and I walk with a limp. The accident was over for her in a week or two, but it will never really be over for me. And seeing her just reminds me of that.

When you reach the legal drinking age, you'll have to decide when to drink and how much you can handle. Obviously, the *only* safe strategy is not to drink at all if you are going to be driving. It's very hard to predict how much alcohol you can drink before your driving is affected, and each person has his own limit. Alcohol can have a very different effect on you than it has on someone else, and the same amount can affect you differently at different times.

IF YOU'VE HAD TOO MUCH

Even though you know better, you may have the opportunity to drink and drive before you are of legal drinking age. Regardless of whether you've been watching what you're drinking or swilling down everything in sight, you may suddenly find to your surprise that you are in no condition to drive. Now what should you do? Some of your options may be embarrassing, but they all beat getting behind the wheel. The simplest choice may be to call a cab to take you home, and then come back the next day to get your car. If you can't get a cab, you can always ask someone with you to drive. However, if you're at a party where everyone is drinking, your friends may not be in any better shape than you are. If there's no one there who can safely drive you home, you're going to have to call someone. This can be your parents, a close friend, the parents of a friend, or another adult, such as an uncle or your basketball coach. Obviously they won't be thrilled that you've gotten yourself in this situation. But as angry as they may be, they'd much rather have you call them than have you get behind the wheel drunk or high.

Unfortunately, many times when you're wrecked, you're the last one to recognize that fact. So if friends tell you that they think you're too drunk to drive, listen to them! It's difficult for many people to confront friends who have had too much to drink. If your friends have worked up the courage to say this to you, you're probably in pretty bad shape.

WHEN YOUR FRIEND IS TOO DRUNK TO DRIVE

One of the trickiest problems associated with drinking and driving is figuring out how to handle someone else who is too drunk to drive. It's usually hard to convince a person that he or she is no longer safe behind the wheel. The issue is even more complicated if this person was supposed to drive you home, as Denise found out.

I went to this party with a guy I was dating at the time. We were both drinking, but he had a lot more than I did. On the way home, he could hardly keep the car on the road. I was really scared and kept asking him to let me drive, but he wouldn't. Finally, when we stopped for a red light, he just passed out. I managed to push him over and get into the driver's seat. But wouldn't you know, less than fifteen minutes later the police stopped me for running a stop sign and wrote me up for DWI. My stupid date didn't get a ticket or anything, even though he was the whole reason I was driving.

One suggestion for avoiding situations like this is to choose a designated driver, a person who agrees not to drink during a party so that he or she can drive others home. This is an excellent idea. However, many things can go wrong with this plan, so don't think that because someone else is the designated driver that this gives you the green light to get wasted. For example, if the designated driver doesn't keep his end of the bargain and gets drunk himself, you're stuck.

It's easier to avoid a dangerous situation than it is to try to get out of one. So always take a good look at the person who will be driving *before* getting in the car, especially when leaving a party. Has he or she been chugging down one beer after the other? Is he slurring his words, staggering, being extremely loud, or just acting weird? These are clear-cut signals *not* to get in the car with this person, but they aren't the only signs that a driver may be impaired. Some people can be very drunk without seeming to be. So regardless of whether the driver looks drunk or not, if you know someone has had more than a drink or two, it's a *terrible* idea to let this person drive you anywhere. Also, if you've been drinking yourself, it may be harder for you to determine whether someone else has had too much. This is another reason why you should go easy on the alcohol even if you're not driving.

A more difficult problem is deciding what to do if you're already in a car with a driver who's drunk. The first step in this situation is to try to get the driver to pull over and let you or someone else drive. Although many impaired drivers are reluctant to do this, some may be aware that they're having trouble and actually be relieved. Of course, this assumes that you or another passenger is in good enough condition to drive. If you can't convince the driver to let someone else drive, the next question is when to just get out of the car. This can be a very tough decision, particularly if it's in the middle of the night and you are in the middle of nowhere. However, if the driver is careening down the wrong side of the road, traveling at very high speeds, or narrowly missing other cars, you may be better off taking your chances outside the car, regardless of where you are. Ask the driver to stop and let you out, preferably at the nearest safe place. If he won't, take the next opportunity—for example, when he stops for gas or at a red light—and just open the door and go.

Having a cell phone with you at all times can make a huge difference in how these scenarios turn out. When her date passed out, Denise would have been much better off if she had just pulled the car over to the side and called someone to come and get them both. And ditching your ride in an unfamiliar area is much less scary—and less risky—if you have a way to contact the police, your parents, or a friend. But if you'd be afraid to call your parents under similar circumstances, be sure to carry the emergency number of someone else with you at all times. It's also a good idea whenever you go out to bring enough money with you to catch a cab, bus, or train home in an emergency.

Drinking while driving, whether you are drunk or not, is illegal everywhere. So is driving while impaired, whether you are actually drinking at the time or not. But other motor vehicle laws related to alcohol can differ drastically from state to state. Some of these laws may be much stricter than you might imagine, so it's a good idea to brush up on these regulations if you plan to drive in another state. For example, in Virginia,

it is illegal to possess alcohol while driving, even if the bottle or can is unopened. Possession is defined as being within your reach. This means that an unopened six-pack in the trunk is OK, while the same six-pack in the passenger seat is not.

ILLEGAL DRUGS

No matter how old you are, having or using illegal drugs is against the law and a bad idea. Driving while under the influence of drugs is even dumber.

This combination is every bit as dangerous and illegal as driving while under the influence of alcohol. In fact, *all* of the problems discussed above concerning alcohol and driving apply to

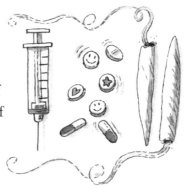

doing drugs and driving. You can also face additional charges for drug possession if the police find drugs on you or in your car. Since your driving will be more erratic if you're stoned, it's more likely that you'll be pulled over. And once the police stop you, chances are good that you and your car will be searched.

SEDATING MEDICATIONS

Alcohol and illegal drugs are not the only things that can affect your ability to drive. There are a number of perfectly legal medications, some

of which can be bought without a prescription, that can also have dangerous effects. Among the most common of these are certain sedating antihistamines used to treat allergies. These drugs can make you very drowsy, as Will discovered firsthand.

> I've got these allergies that come on in the fall, right at the beginning of football season. The year I made starting quarterback was also a big year for ragweed. What with my eyes itching and tearing, my nose running, and me sneezing all the time, I could hardly play. I started taking some over-the-counter allergy pills, but they made me really sleepy. One afternoon when I was driving home from school, I dozed off and crashed into a telephone pole. The impact broke my arm in two places. Everyone said I was lucky, but it didn't feel that way—I was out for every single game that year.

Not all people respond to sedating antihistamines by becoming sleepy. But these drugs are especially unsafe because they can impair your reaction time and decision-making ability *without* making you drowsy. As a result, you may not be aware that you are affected. The consequences are nothing to sneeze at, however. The effect of these antihistamines on driving ability is similar to the effect of blood alcohol levels of .05 percent. Because of this, most states have laws against driving under the influence of any drug that impairs driving, including sedating antihistamines.

There are plenty of nonsedating allergy medications on the market. While they may be more expensive, they are definitely safer. Many prescription drugs are also sedating, and have warnings to that effect on the bottle. Other medications, such as cough syrups, may contain narcotics. Swigging down these drugs can also reduce your ability to drive safely. When you have a cold, the flu, or allergies, you're not at your best anyway—driving while taking medications for these conditions makes things even worse.

Getting a Ticket

It's a beautiful day and you're driving along, enjoying the scenery. Suddenly, out of nowhere, flashing lights appear behind you, and a police officer signals you to pull over. Or maybe you know left turns are prohibited at this corner, but there's no one around, everyone does it anyway, and besides, you're late and this will save time. As luck would have it, you're not as alone as you thought. A police cruiser is lurking around the corner, waiting to nab drivers who turn.

Whether you know exactly why you've been pulled over or you don't have a clue what you might have done wrong, being stopped by the police makes most people feel nervous, intimidated, and defensive. So while the officer is walking over to your car, take a deep breath and collect yourself. And forget those fantasies of charming the cop into forgetting the ticket. In the vast majority of cases, this is not going to happen. In fact, there is very little that you can do at this point to change his mind if the officer has decided to give you a summons. However, there are plenty of things you can do to make things worse. To avoid digging yourself deeper into a hole, keep the following tips in mind.

BE RESPECTFUL

When dealing with the police, be polite, produce the documents asked for, and answer the officer's questions honestly. Then shut up. Pleading, offering excuses, or claiming that it's the town's fault because the sign wasn't clear is highly unlikely to cause the officer to decide you don't deserve that ticket after all. Since these responses suggest that

you aren't willing to take responsibility for your actions, they actually increase your chance of being ticketed. Being arrogant, argumentative, defiant, sarcastic, or just plain obnoxious is even worse, and may cause the officer to look for additional reasons to ticket you.

DON'T TRY TO BE SLICK

Harry has been a highway patrolman for over thirty years, and he's seen young drivers do incredibly stupid things to avoid getting a summons.

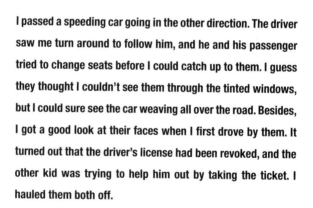

> I passed a speeding car going in the other direction. The driver saw me turn around to follow him, and he and his passenger tried to change seats before I could catch up to them. I guess they thought I couldn't see them through the tinted windows, but I could sure see the car weaving all over the road. Besides, I got a good look at their faces when I first drove by them. It turned out that the driver's license had been revoked, and the other kid was trying to help him out by taking the ticket. I hauled them both off.

Harry's advice to all drivers is simple: "Don't try to fool the cops. We've seen practically everything at least once, so we have a pretty good idea of the things people are likely to try. It's not going to work, and it can only get you further in trouble."

FIGHTING A TICKET

Of course, police officers aren't gods, and like everyone else, they make mistakes. If you truly feel that the officer shouldn't have ticketed you, fight the ticket in traffic court, not on the side of the road. Having to appear in court is inconvenient and time-consuming, and there's no guarantee that you'll win. But there are some things you can do to increase your chance of success. For exam-ple, if you missed a stop sign because it was partially hidden behind an overgrown bush, bring a photograph of this to show the judge. In fact, just showing up at court may be enough. In some places the ticketing officer is required to appear as well. If he or she fails to do so, your ticket will usually be dismissed.

SALVAGING YOUR DRIVING RECORD

Fighting a summons in court may seem like more trouble than it's worth. But a ticket for a moving violation—particularly speeding—can cost you a lot more than the fine, especially if you are a young driver. Even one speeding ticket can result in a huge increase in your insurance rates. In addition, a traffic conviction adds points on your driving record—too many points and you can lose your license. So anything you can do to wipe the ticket off your record is worth a try.

Fortunately, getting the ticket dismissed in court may not be the only way of doing this. In some states you can ask that a ticket for a minor moving violation be dismissed if you haven't had a vehicle-related violation in the previous three years. In other states a minor speeding conviction can be erased from your record if you take a safety course for drivers. Your state's Department of Motor Vehicles or your local traffic court can tell you what steps you can take to clean up your driving record.

Breakdowns

There are countless ways that your car can break down. You can handle some of these breakdowns—such as those caused by a dead battery or a flat tire—by yourself if you have the right equipment. But in most cases, you'll need a mechanic's help. The amount of grief these more serious situations will cause you depends largely on two things—whether you have a cell phone (or are near a pay phone) and whether you belong to an organization that provides emergency road service.

If your car won't start at all, there's a good chance your battery is dead. An engine that turns over once or twice but doesn't catch or just groans when you turn on the ignition is a good sign that this is the problem.

You may be able to recharge the battery yourself if you have jumper cables and access to another car. If you are at home or in your neighborhood, call your parents or a friend and ask them to drive over with a car to use as a booster. Even if you can't reach anyone you know, other motorists will usually be willing to help you with their car.

Instructions for working jumper cables are given below. Using them is easy, but they must be attached correctly, so read the directions carefully.

Of course, other things besides a dead battery can cause a car not to start. In this case, you'll have to have your car towed to a garage to be repaired. Hopefully, you belong to one of the many emergency road services available. If so, call

them for help. If not, you're going to have to find a local garage that will tow your car away. If you are near home, you can always call your parents and ask them to look in the phone book and either call a garage for you or give you a few phone numbers you can try. If you are in another area, you'll have to try to find a phone book yourself to look for a towing service. If all else fails, call the local police. They may be able to give you the number of a garage that will help you.

HOW TO USE JUMPER CABLES

- Move the two cars close enough so that the cables can stretch from the battery in your car to the battery in the booster car, *but be sure the two vehicles are not touching.*
- Turn off all unnecessary lights, radios, etc., in both vehicles.
- Attach the clamps of the jumper cables *in this order:*
  - First, attach one clamp of a cable to the positive (+) post of your battery. (The positive post is the one that is colored red.)
  - Then, attach the other end of the *same* cable to the positive (+) post of the booster battery.
  - Next, take the other cable and attach one clamp to the negative (−) post of the booster battery. (The negative post is the black one.)

- Finally, attach the end of that cable to a solid metal part of your engine, away from the battery. (Do not connect the cable to any moving part.)
- Start the engine of the booster car and let it run for a few minutes at a fast idle, about 2,000 rpm, if it has a tachometer, to make sure that the battery is fully charged.
- Turn the key to start your engine. Once it starts, leave the jumper cables connected and let your engine run at a fast idle, about 2,000 rpm, for several minutes.
- Carefully remove the cables in the reverse order that you attached them (starting with the negative cables first).

Caution: The gas produced by charging a battery is highly explosive. Do not smoke or allow a spark or open flame anywhere near either car while you are doing this.

HOW TO USE A PORTABLE CHARGER

- Turn off your ignition.
- Attach the positive (+) cable to the positive (+) post of your battery first, then attach the negative (−) cable to a solid metal part of your engine.
- Turn on your ignition and your car should start.
- Remove the negative cable first, then the positive cable.

FLAT TIRE

Another common cause of breakdowns is a flat tire. As in the case of a dead battery, a flat tire is something you can fix on your own. Unlike dead batteries, however, flats often happen in very inconvenient places. If you have a blowout, the popping sound and a sudden sagging on one side of the car will tell you exactly what has happened. In less dramatic instances a *flop-flop* sound will let you know you've got a flat. In either case, continue driving straight ahead. Take your foot off the gas and let the car slow down. Wait until you've reached a safe speed before braking or trying to pull off the road, as you may lose control of the car otherwise. Occasionally, flats caused by a slow leak may not be obvious at first. If the car seems lower on one side or handles differently somehow, slow down carefully, pull over, and check your tires.

If you have an inflated spare tire, a jack, and a lug wrench, you're in business. Changing a tire is easy, but again, follow the instructions below carefully. If you don't have the equipment to change your tire, you'll have to call your emergency road service or a tow truck.

HOW TO CHANGE A TIRE

- Pull well off the road and onto a level area if possible.
- Put the car in park and apply the parking brake. If your car has a manual transmission, put the car in reverse or first gear. Put on your hazard lights.

- Take out the spare tire, the jack, and the lug wrench.
- Remove the hubcap if there is one on the wheel. (You can pop it off with a screwdriver or the jack handle.)
- Before trying to lift the car up with the jack, loosen each lug nut one turn counterclockwise while the car is still on the ground. (The lug nuts are the bolts that attach the wheel to the car.)
- Place the jack under a reinforced section of the body of the car. Your owner's manual will tell you where these sections are.
- Jack the car up until the flat tire is a few inches off the ground.
- Remove the lug nuts and take the wheel off.
- Place the spare tire on the axle, and line the holes up with the posts.
- Put the lug nuts back on and tighten them lightly.
- Lower the car and remove the jack.
- Tighten the lug nuts firmly.
- The first chance you get, have your flat repaired or replaced and put it back on the car. Stow your spare away in the trunk. If you have one of the small doughnut spares, remember—these are not like regular tires. They are intended for emergency use only and are not meant to be driven over long distances.

Caution: Never place your hands or feet under the wheel of the car once it has been raised. If the car slips off the jack, it might fall on you. Also, be extremely careful when changing a tire on the side of the road. Many roads have narrow shoulders that barely give you enough room to get your car off the pavement, much less to stand next to it and work. Changing a tire with your butt jutting into the road is literally an accident waiting to happen. Even if you are off the pavement, be very aware of traffic on your side of the road, since drivers may not see you hunched down by the wheel.

OVERHEATED CAR

In terms of hassles and expense, an overheated car falls somewhere in between dead batteries and flat tires on the one hand and much bigger problems on the other. Just how much trouble you're in depends on what caused your car to overheat.

There can be a number of reasons why this has happened. The ones that you may have a chance of fixing are (1) you've run out of coolant, or (2) coolant is not reaching the engine, either because a hose has sprung a leak or one of the clamps attaching the hose has come loose.

A temperature gauge that is well into the red danger zone and steam pouring out from under your hood are two signs of an overheated engine. If you see either of these, pull over to the side of the road as soon as possible, put on your emergency flashers, turn off the engine, and let the car cool down for at least fifteen to twenty minutes. Then look for the cause of the problem.

To check the coolant level, look on the side of the plastic coolant reservoir. The level of coolant should be between the low and the full lines on the reservoir. If your coolant level is too low and you have coolant and water with you (or can find some), replace the coolant. Never add coolant by itself. If you don't know the exact proportions of water and coolant, a 50-50 mix will generally work. If nothing seems to be wrong with the coolant level, inspect your hoses for leaks. You may be able to patch a hole, split, or crack in the hose if you can get your hands on some duct tape. If the hoses themselves seem okay, tighten any loose clamps. If there's nothing wrong with your coolant level or your hoses—or if there is, but you can't fix the problem—then you're going to have to call a garage to tow you.

BIGGER, BADDER BREAKDOWNS

Unfortunately, many breakdowns are not as easily handled as those resulting from a dead battery, flat tire, or over-heated car. If you know what to do, however, you can get off the road safely and get help.

Usually you'll get at least a few minutes' warning that your car is about to die. For example, smoke may start pouring out from under the hood, your car may start to slow down, or weird sounds may start coming from the engine. You may not have much time before your car loses power, so use it to get over to the side of the road as quickly as possible.

Pull off the pavement and turn on your hazard lights. Then, take a deep breath, calm down, and assess your situation. Are you safely off the road? If not, you and your passengers need to get out of the car, *assuming you can do so without getting hit by traffic.* For example, if your car has stalled in the middle lane on a freeway, getting out of the car is riskier than staying put. But in this case, be doubly sure that your hazard lights are on. Do you see flames anywhere? If so, you'll need to get out of the car.

Otherwise, stay in the car and call your emergency road service (or the police if you don't have one) on your cell phone. Give your parents or a friend a call too so that someone knows what's happened and can come and get you, since neither the police nor the emergency road service will drive you home. Then wait.

If you don't have a cell phone with you or you can't get a signal, your options will depend on where you are. If you are on a road that is regularly patrolled by the police, such as a freeway or beltway, a squad car will eventually come by and help you. Otherwise, if you are in a populated area, lock your car and walk to the nearest store, gas station, or restaurant that has a phone. In a more rural area you may have to go to a house and ask to use a phone.

Another alternative is to accept help from a passing motorist. Be very careful how you do this, however! Not everyone who stops to help someone who's had a breakdown has good intentions. In fact, some may be dangerous predators. A good rule of thumb is *never* to get into a car with strangers. Instead, ask if you can borrow their cell phone to call for help, or ask them to stop at a gas station and call for you.

Finally, it is possible that you may be stuck in a

completely deserted area with no access to a phone and no motorists passing by. In this case, it's best to stay where you are and wait for someone to find you. This is one reason why it's always a good idea to tell your parents where you are going and when you expect to be back. Then if your car breaks down and you have no way of getting help, at least they will know where to start looking for you.

EMERGENCY ROAD SERVICES

There are many organizations, such as AAA, that provide emergency road service for a low yearly membership fee. Although these services may vary somewhat, at a minimum they generally include minor mechanical repairs to get your car back on the road: charging your battery, changing a flat tire (if you provide the spare), supplying you with a limited amount of fuel if you've run out of gas, and towing your car to the nearest participating garage if it can't be easily fixed on the spot. Even if you never need to use the service, the fee is well worth the security of knowing you can always get help if necessary. So if you aren't already covered by your parents' membership in one of these programs, join one yourself.

Keep in mind, however, that these emergency services are not intended to substitute for regular maintenance. There is a limit to the number of times you can call to have them charge an old battery, for example, before they refuse. And remember, it doesn't matter how good an emergency road service is if you don't have a way to contact them. So always carry your cell phone with you whenever you get in the car. You never know when you may need it.

AVOIDING BREAKDOWNS

The best way to deal with breakdowns is to prevent them in the first place. Lindsey's parents gave her a car and paid for the insurance. But they told her that maintenance was her responsibility.

I thought I was doing pretty good because I had my oil changed every now and then and checked to make sure my tires weren't going bald. But I sort of forgot about the other stuff. After all, I figured if my car passed inspection, then it must be in good shape.

As she found out, that was no guarantee that everything was all right.

I was coming home from visiting my boyfriend at college when all of a sudden my car lost power. I was barely able to coast off the road. Luckily, I was on the turnpike because I didn't have a cell phone. I put my hood up and turned on my flashers, and pretty soon a highway patrolman came by and called AAA for me.

The problem was a simple one, but fixing it was not.

My drive belt broke. Unfortunately, the garage didn't carry any replacements that were the right size, so they had to order it. When they told me it would take a couple of days at least, I freaked! I was in the middle of nowhere, and there wasn't a motel for miles—not that I had any intention of staying there. I had to take a three-hour bus ride home to Philadelphia, then take the same bus ride back to the garage the next week to pick up my car.

Of course, not all breakdowns can be prevented. But if Lindsey had been more careful about regular maintenance, she could have avoided this one. In addition to maintaining your car, it's a good idea to take some extra precautions before setting out on any long trip. To be safe, check your oil, transmission, brakes, and coolant level, as well as your hoses, belts, and tires. If you spot any problems—or if something just seems strange—take your car to a mechanic and have it looked at before you start out.

19

Accidents

Whether it's a minor fender bender or a four-car collision, being in an accident is traumatic, to say the least. If you're like most people in this situation, you'll probably find it hard to think clearly, especially if you or someone else has been hurt. So learning ahead of time how to respond will be extremely important in protecting your safety and that of your passengers, as well as preserving your good driving record and low insurance rate.

PEOPLE FIRST,
PROPERTY SECOND

The first and most important thing in any accident is to determine whether or not someone has been hurt. If so, getting medical attention will take precedence over everything else. If your car can still be driven, move it to the side of the road. Then call 911 and explain what has happened. If someone has been injured,  the dispatcher will send both an ambulance and a squad car to the scene. If you can't move your car and it's sitting in the middle of the road, ask any passengers who aren't hurt to exit and move to a safe place *if they can do so without running the risk of being hit by traffic.* Do not try to move anyone who is hurt, as you may cause further injury to them.

EXCHANGING INFORMATION

The next step is to exchange names, addresses, driver's licenses, and insurance information with the driver of the other car. This is extremely important! Do not let the other driver leave without providing this information. If he or she attempts

to go without doing so, try to get the license-plate number of the car. Also, be very careful what you say and do *not* admit blame, even if you think the accident may be partly your fault. This is not to suggest that you should try to avoid responsibility, just that your words may be twisted and/or used against you at a later date.

THE POLICE

Most states, as well as your insurance company, require you to file a police report, even for minor accidents, so stay at the scene until the police arrive. Make a note of the name of the police officer, and be sure that he has heard your version of what occurred. Again, tell the officer what happened, but do not admit fault.

YOUR INSURANCE COMPANY

Notify your insurance company about the accident as soon as you can, *whether or not you plan to make a claim for damages.* If the cost of repairing your car is less than the increase in insurance rates that may result from making a claim, you may be tempted to pay for the repairs yourself and not say anything to your insurance company. But just because you don't intend to make a claim does *not* mean that you don't have to notify your insurance company. The other driver (or even one of your passengers) may try to collect from your insurance company for medical expenses or property damage. Not telling your insurance company about the accident may result in their refusing to pay any claims that result or refusing to defend you in court.

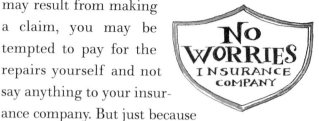

The only time you should even consider not reporting the accident to your insurance company is if *all* of the following are true: yours was the only car involved; you were the only person in the car; no one was hurt, including yourself or any bystanders; there was no damage to any other public or private property; and the police were not called.

Finally, if you were driving a car that is not yours, it goes without saying that you *must* tell the owner about the accident as soon as possible so that it can be reported to his or her insurance company.

A WORD ABOUT
NO-FAULT INSURANCE

No-fault insurance does *not* mean that it doesn't matter whose fault an accident is. It merely means that your insurance company will pay for your expenses (up to the limit of your coverage)  regardless of whether or not you were to blame. If the accident was your fault, your insurance premium will usually increase and the other driver's insurance company will probably seek repayment from your company for their client's expenses. If the other driver was at fault, that person's rate will increase and your company will seek repayment from his or her insurance company.

DON'T GET TAKEN FOR A RIDE

Occasionally, one of the drivers involved in an accident may suggest to the other that they not report the accident to the police or their insurance companies. Usually, the proposal sounds something like this: "Look, it's only a few dents, and it'll probably cost us both more in increased insurance premiums than it will to pay for these minor repairs. We've each got about the same amount of damage, so let's just let it go and not report it." Or: "Gosh, I'm really sorry! This was all my fault, and I'll certainly pay to have your car repaired. But I really don't need another ticket on my record, so let's not report it. Here's my name and address. Get an itemized estimate from a couple of garages, and I'll send you a check immediately."

Generally, people make suggestions like these because (1) they have no insurance (or perhaps no driver's license) and thus don't want to get the police involved, (2) they know the accident was their fault and are trying to talk you out of making an insurance claim against them, and/or (3) they have no intention of paying you anything. If the accident was not your fault, your insurance rate usually will not go up. So anyone who suggests not reporting it to avoid an increase in premiums probably thinks the accident was his or her fault. Under these circumstances it may make sense for him to pay for his own repairs, but why should you foot the bill for yours? Rest assured, if he thought the accident was your fault, there would be no mention of insurance premiums going up "for both of us," and he'd be more than willing to have your insurance pay for those "minor repairs." And if you let someone leave the scene of an accident with only a promise to reimburse you, you can be guaranteed you'll never hear from him again. Even if he gave you his real name and address, you have no way to prove he was even involved in the accident, much less that he owes you money.

Unfortunately, because of your age, other drivers involved in an accident with you may try to take advantage of you, attempting to bully you into admitting blame or trying to convince you not to report the accident. It's easy to get rattled in a situation like this, so take a deep breath and try to stay calm. If you're feeling pressured by the other driver, tell him that your parents have a rule that any conversations about these matters be with them, not you.

All drivers should play by the book when it comes to dealing with an accident, but sticking to the rules provides special protection for young drivers. Don't let someone con you into doing otherwise.

DEALING WITH YOUR PARENTS

How your parents respond to the fact that you've had an accident will depend on several things. Obviously, their reaction is likely to be different if you

Hello? Hello?

were drunk, sped through a red light, and slammed into an-other car than if you were waiting for a traffic light to change when someone rear-ended you. But whether it was your fault or not, one thing is sure—the accident is bound to have scared them. Rick's mother may have overreacted, but most parents can identify with her feelings.

I tried not to show it, but I always worried whenever Rick took the car. I kept telling myself that he was a good driver and that I was being overprotective, but I was always a nervous wreck until he got home. The night of the accident, he and a friend had gone to a club. The phone rang about eleven, and the minute I heard his friend's voice, I knew something terrible had happened. When he said they'd had an accident and he was calling from the hospital, I started shaking so hard I could barely hold the phone. All I could think was, "I'm going to lose my child! He's going to die!" The ride to the hospital seemed to take forever! When I walked into the emergency room, Rick was sitting there getting stitches in his arm. I was so relieved that he was alive and not seriously hurt that I burst into tears and started wailing. Rick and his friend just stared at me in amazement. They thought I was upset about the stitches and couldn't understand my reaction. Evidently, his friend told me on the phone that Rick had gotten a gash on his arm but was okay otherwise. I guess I was so upset that I didn't even hear that.

If the accident was not your fault, your driving privileges probably will not be affected. Even if you did do something wrong, your parents are likely to recognize that anyone—especially a new driver—can make a mistake. If you have been a responsible driver in the past, were honest with them about the accident, and have not broken the driving contract you made with them, chances are that their main concern will be that you've learned from your mistake.

On the other hand, if you caused an accident by doing something that you knew was illegal and/or dangerous, your parents may decide to revoke some of your driving privileges, such as using the car at night, or they may not allow you to drive at all. In this case, you'll have to regain their trust before they'll feel comfortable letting you behind the wheel again.

LONG-TERM EFFECTS

Many accidents continue to affect the people involved long after the cars have been towed away.

It goes without saying that an accident in which someone was killed or left handicapped has permanent consequences. But even if the accident was a minor one and no one was hurt, the effects can still be long lasting. For one thing, having an accident can really shake your confidence.

In Keisha's case, the accident wasn't even her fault—and that was part of the problem.

If I had done something wrong, then I could have learned not to do that again. But I can't do anything about the stuff other people do.

The van that struck her car had come from the right. From then on, she swerved every time a car approached her from that direction.

I'd see a car on my right, and without even looking, I'd pull way over to the left. Finally, I thought, "Forget it! I'm going to have another accident if this keeps up. I'm just not going to drive anymore!"

Fortunately, Keisha's father was able to help her.

My dad was great! He told me that lots of people feel this way after an accident. He said that it was like being thrown from a horse—to get over it, you had to get back on the horse again. So he sat beside me while I tried driving in my neighborhood, where there's not much traffic and everyone goes pretty slowly. When I got so I could see a car coming from the right without swerving, we went to more crowded areas. It took a couple of weeks, but I'm okay driving just about anywhere now. I don't think I could have done it, though, if he hadn't been there with me.

If the accident was more serious and you or someone else was hurt, you may be left with feelings that are much harder to deal with. Anger, either at yourself or another person, is a very common reaction to having been injured, especially if this has left you disfigured or disabled. Having caused an accident in which someone else was hurt or killed leaves most people feeling extremely guilty, but you don't have to have been responsible for the accident to feel this way. James was in the backseat when the car he was in skidded off the road and into a tree. Of the three young men in the car, he was the only one to survive.

I kept asking myself, "Why me? Why was I the only one who didn't die?" Every time I saw their parents, I kept thinking, "They must hate me! I know they wish it had been me and not their kid."

Regardless of whether you were responsible or not, any accident that results in the loss of someone or something important to you is likely to make you feel sad. Sorrow and grief over someone who died, a friendship that will never be the same again, or the life you might have had if you hadn't been hurt are all normal reactions. But sometimes these emotions can seem overwhelming. Whatever you are feeling, talking about what you are going through can be a big help in dealing with your emotions after an accident. If you're having problems coping with your feelings, tell your parents, your school counselor, or another adult you trust so that you can get help.

Helping Others

Just as it's important to know what to do if you have a breakdown or an accident, you'll also want to know what steps to take if you come across another driver who's run into a serious problem.

STRANDED MOTORIST

There she is—standing helplessly on the side of the road, the hood of her car up and steam pouring out of the engine. She waves to flag you down. Should you pull over and help her?

Yes and no. Of course, you'll help. But sadly,

stopping is not a good idea, particularly if you are a young driver, and especially if you are alone. Unfortunately, there is always a possibility that the accident has been 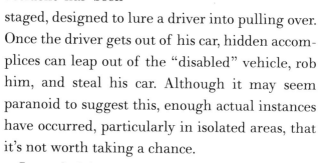 staged, designed to lure a driver into pulling over. Once the driver gets out of his car, hidden accomplices can leap out of the "disabled" vehicle, rob him, and steal his car. Although it may seem paranoid to suggest this, enough actual instances have occurred, particularly in isolated areas, that it's not worth taking a chance.

Instead, drive to a place where you can safely pull over and use your cell phone to call the police. If you don't have a phone with you, stop at the nearest gas station, store, or restaurant and call from there.

WITNESSING AN ACCIDENT

Witnessing an accident, whether it's already occurred or happens in front of your eyes, is always upsetting. Even if no one ap-

pears to be seriously hurt, it's a scary reminder of how quickly things can go wrong. What you should do when you see an accident depends primarily on whether help is already on the way or whether you are the first on the scene.

If there are others already helping the victims—such as police, emergency medical personnel, or even other motorists—your job is to keep moving so you don't cause additional pileups. Often, drivers passing by can be so busy rubbernecking that they rear-end the car in front of them, so keep your eyes on the road ahead.

On the other hand, if you are the first on the scene, you'll want to help if you can. But there is a right way and a wrong way of doing this. The most important step in aiding the accident victims is not to become one yourself. First, pull over in a safe place and call the police. (If you don't have a cell phone, drive immediately to the nearest house, store, gas station, or other place that has a phone and call from there.) Next, try to help anyone who is in obvious danger, but *not* at the risk of your own life or safety. For example, difficult as it may be, you should not approach a car that is in flames. The chances are just too great that it may explode. You should also not try to move someone, as this may result in spinal-cord injuries that can leave the person paralyzed. The only exception may be if you are certified in giving CPR and the accident victim has stopped breathing or has no pulse.

There are several simple steps you can take that can be very helpful, however. Often, people involved in an accident are dazed and disoriented, and may place themselves in further danger by wandering onto the road, and so on. You can help them get to a safe place and see that they stay put. If the driver is unconscious or hurt, you can also take charge of any uninjured children or pets in the car. Finally, just knowing that someone has stopped to help and will stay until medical assistance arrives can be enormously reassuring to a person who has been injured.

Keep in Mind . . .

As more experienced drivers will tell you, learning to drive will take the rest of your life. The more time you spend in the driver's seat, the more skilled—and more comfortable—you'll become. But you'll find there's always something new to learn. Some emergency road services, such as AAA, publish magazines and sponsor Web sites for their members with tips about driving and car maintenance, as well as other topics. Your insurance company may also offer videos or other information about driving safely. Take advantage of these opportunities. The more you know, the safer—and more fun—your time behind the wheel will be.

Index